Athelney and Other Poems

Eliza Down

BIBLIOBAZAAR

ATHELNEY

And other Poems.

INCLUDING KENWITH.

BY

ELIZA DOWN.

LONDON:

GEORGE BELL AND SONS, YORK STREET,

COVENT GARDEN.

1884.

TO

W. F. ROCK, ESQ.,

OF HYDE CLIFF, BLACKHEATH,

TO WHOSE KINDNESS THE WRITER IS GREATLY INDEBTED,

This Volume

IS INSCRIBED WITH SENTIMENTS OF SINCERE
GRATITUDE AND ESTEEM.

Torrington, August, 1884.

CONTENTS.

CONTENTS.

ATHELNEY.

PART I.

ING ALFRED came from battle, with his
    thanes
To Chippenham ; where stayed that day
    the Queen
Alswitha, guarded of a few, that yet
Clave to their lord the King, when all his best
Forsook him.   He had passed in arms, to meet
The heathen lances, counting scarce a tithe
Their number, and returned with scarce a tithe
Of those he led to battle.

                    The grey day
Was near its close, but ere its sun, which then,[1]
Wheeled on the lowest pathway of the year,
Sank into darkness, his great shield-like orb

Burned with an angry glare, beneath a pile
Of granite clouds, dark as great boulders strewn
Upon some rugged coast, washed by stern seas,
And kindling them, shot high above their ridge
Great tongues of flame, as if the sulphurous bowels
Of some fierce Etna heaved their vomit up,
Splattering the heavens with fire.   And Avon, looped
About the old vill of the Saxon kings,
Incarnadined beneath that lurid sky,
And ran blood-red ; dark as the streams which flowed
From the great wine-press of the wrath of God,
Seen by the Seer of Patmos, the red blood
Of the great grapes of the earth's vine, full-ripe,
Trodden in the press, which flowed far out and deep,
Reaching e'en to the bridles of the horse
Of vision.[2]

          So the sullen heavens, fire-flushed
With that wild sunset, cast their glare on tower
And gate, as Alfred entered Chippenham,
Returning from the fatal battle-field.
Then said the King : "This kingdom which I raised
From out its ruins,[3] falls this hour again

To ruin, and the bestial lives in man,
And everywhere the heathen works his will !"

And when the night darkened with heavy shades
The ancient vill, King Alfred called to him
His servant Ethelnoth,[4] and gave him charge
To lead the Queen to some secure retreat ;
Where hidden from the heathen, she might dwell
In secrecy, attended of a few,
The tried retainers of his house.   " Arise,
Haste on your journey," said the King, " and when
Your business is accomplished come to me
Within the woods of Somerset whither I go
To seek a refuge from mine enemies."
So gave command the King, whereat the group
Of trembling women, huddled round the Queen,
Lifted their voice, and wept aloud ; but she,
Like some great grandeur of the antique stone,
A sculptured Pallas or Minerva, stood
In utter stillness, mute and motionless :
Only the blood-red rubies on her breast
Flashed with a sudden throbbing of the heart,

Betraying her emotion ; and the King
Turned, and his eyes were full of heavy tears,
Ready to fall, as he addressed his thanes :
"The hour is bitter, but we needs must bend
To that high Will which shapes our destiny.
Despair not wholly ; though I go from hence
To solitary sojourn in the wilds,
Yet have I hope to raise my arm once more
Against the troublers of my country's peace,
Those that have wrought this ruin. Ye, my thanes,
Slack not endeavour, bate no jot of faith,
Fulfil your part, I mine. Ah, noble thanes,
Think of that field of Ashdune,⁶ where we strove,
Until we threw the northern kings, and like
A mountain torrent smitten into mists
Upon the jutty points of mighty rocks,
Headlong they fled. So will we fight again,
And heave and oust these pagans. Now farewell,
Farewell, keep you my charge religiously,
As ye shall answer in that dreadful hour
When we shall stand at feet of the High God,
To give account each of himself to God."

So spake the King, and added not, but turned
Toward the silent Queen.   And Ethelnoth,
Passing from out the hall, said to a thane
That went with him, " Mark the King's countenance !
Know I have seen him throned within this hall,
Delivering his judgments to his poor,[6]
And thought him grand, but never saw him grand
As now."

         And Alfred took within his hands,
Alswitha's hands, his wife, and tenderly
Kissed them, but spoke no word, nor she to him,
Only her glorious eyes, suddenly raised,
Shed into his their effluence, pure light
Of the clear spirit.   Thus awhile they stood
A little moment, and then slowly drew
Their hands asunder, and so turned to part,
Ending their silent farewell.

                Then drew near
The weeping women of the Queen and brought
The two fair children of Alswitha,[7] whom
The King, their father, took within his arms
And kissed, and blessed ; and when the brief and sad

Caress was ended, the pale Queen arose,
And leading the young children by the hand
Passed forth, her maidens following her steps,
And thence in care of Ethelnoth the Earl,
With a small band of chosen men for guard,
Departed.

       And the servants of the King
Went each his way according as he bade,
And after them the King went forth alone,
And to the woody wilds of Somerset
Repairing, there within the solitudes
Made his abode in secret.

       And the Jarls
Who led the Danish army came, and seized
The vill of Chippenham, making their camp
Where Alfred dwelt, and from the ruined halls
Of the West Saxon ruler issuing, spread
Ruin around.   The bands of ancient law
Were loosed, and everywhere in all the realm
Th' anarchic heads of violence raised themselves
Unsmitten.   The vexed land groaned with its woes,
And desolate and trodden down, unkinged,

ATHELNEY.

Unpeopled, and dismantled of its forts,
Lay at the mercy of the heathen foe.

    *   *   *   *   *

Belted with the impenetrable woods,
Near to the mingling of the rivers Thone
And Parret, lay a marshy island, grown
With alder and with willow ; all about,
A hundred oozy streams went meandering,
Knotted around the place like a thick coil
Of snakelings.   Thither the unsceptred King,
Fleeing his enemies, had come, and there
Sheltered unknown within a neat-herd's house,
Hiding his kinghood 'neath a peasant's garb,
And as a peasant working with his hands
Gave service to the man beneath whose roof
He lodged.

              And when Earl Ethelnoth had brought
The Queen Alswitha on her way, he came
To seek his lord, as he had bidden him
Within the ancient forest.

                   A hoar gloom
Enwrapped the labyrinthic paths, o'er-hung

With boughs of lichened trees, oaks gaunt and grey,
Whose rungs of root made rough the ground below.
The wintry noon within those doleful shades
Was as the twilight wan.   Deep silence reigned,
Save for a solitary heron's cry,
Or the shrill note of the wild fowl that rose
From reedy margin of the sluggish streams,
Scared by th' intruder's step.
                                    And Ethelnoth
Came to the morass-compassed isle, since named
As Athelney, where in the neat-herd's house
The King lay hidden ; 'mid the great dark coils
Of slowly-flowing water the lone isle,
Covered with rankest woody growth, stretched wide,
Bare of all sign of habitation save
A solitary cottage in the midst,
The forester's abode, which on a slope
Of rising ground appeared, with a dark cirque
Of rugged trees behind.   Toward this the Earl
Directed then his steps, but ere he passed
The oozy shallows where the rushes spread
Their yellow tufts, meshed with the long marsh-grass

ATHELNEY.

That waved above the stream, beheld far off
A man advancing from the thicket side,
With heavy axe across his shoulder slung,
A churl or woodman, such the rustic dress
Proclaimed him, but more nearly viewed, his form,
Warlike and princely, proved him other far
Than that he seemed ; and Ethelnoth strait knew
Under the veil of lowlihood the King,
His master. " Ah, my lord Alfred," he said,
Now near approached, " to meet you here and thus,
Brings to mine eyes th' unusual tears ! " He knelt,
And reverent kissed his royal master's hand,
And flashing into passionate speech : " O King,
Who in thy time of trouble hast put on
The likeness of a servant, thou shalt yet
Stand in thy proper greatness, lord of men,
And put thy feet upon thine enemies' necks ! "

Then he who had borne rule in England said :
" Most king, most servant ; dream not thou, O Earl
Of any lordship else for us, save that
Which largeliest wears the form of service." " Sire,

The Ealdor made reply, "servant or lord,
Even as it pleases you to name yourself,
Yet shall, my liege, in happier days to come,
The worship of your people compass you,
As the great heavens encircle earth, who now
Are throneless, homeless, friendless!"

                                        Then the Earl
Told how he had fulfilled his charge, and led
The Queen his lady, and the princely babes
Her children, to the appointed bourne, their place
Of hiding.

             "Thanks," said Alfred.   "O my friend,
You crown the perfect service of past years
With this most perfect act of service now
To my beloved ones."

                      "Sire, my gentle liege,
My dearest services have even been
But mean interpreters of the great love
I bear you."

             Then to him, Alfred the king:
"What of my kingdom's fate, O earl?   The Danes
Have seized our vill of Chippenham."   "Ay, King,

And settle there, thick as the loathsome swarm
Of frogs the Seer's uplifted rod of old
Brought on the land of Pharaoh, when they croaked
And leaped in Egypt's ancient palaces,
And on the altars of her idols.   Thick !
They are everywhere ; you cannot move for them,
They fill the land ! "

                Low on the fallen trunk
Of an old tree that stretched along the ground
They sat and talked, the Ealdor and the King ;
And in the silence of the sombre day
Was heard the raven flapping on the wing,
And the low plashing of the sullen streams,
All shagged with sedge about their borders.   "See,"
Said Alfred, "mark this spot, moated and fossed
By Nature's hand.   No meeter site can be
For a rude fort ; impregnably girt
With these thick woods, a few brave men might here
Hold out against great thousands.   Go thou, Earl,
And bid my thanes they hither come to me.
Protected by these woody covertures
Here will we dwell, until I draw the sword

From out the scabbard yet once more, to smite
These heathen ravagers.   Go now thy ways,
Watch what is doing of the enemy,
And bring me tidings speedily ; farewell."

So parted they, there in the desolate woods,—
The Earl retraced the gloomy forest paths,
And Alfred turned again to his abode
Within the marsh-bound isle.

                              There did the King
Tarry unknown, the circle of a moon,
From the thin crescent pale, orbed in its course,
To the broad shield, and then the lessened disc
Nightly diminished, nor disclosed himself
To them with whom he dwelt, so did it chance,
The woodman's wife * looked on him as her thrall,
Not weening of his hidden majesty,
And he full patiently, used to command,
Humbled him to obey, nor grudged to do
The menial task.   Yet did they blindly feel,
The uncouth forester and his rude wife,
A sort of greatness in the man they housed,

And looking on the grandeur of the brow,
Shadowed with sorrow, marvelled in their hearts,
But did not shape their wonder into words,
To question him.

              And Ethelnoth, the earl,
Returned, and with him came a little band,
The remnant of the King's devoted thanes.
They with their lord, within the forest heart,
Made their abode, and gave him service true.
Thence from their secret hold he led them forth,
And smiting oft the spearmen of the Danes,
Roving in scattered bands, drew back again
To covert.   On the borders of the isle
Of Athelney, upon a crag⁹ whose base
The waters washed where they conjoined, the Thone
And Parret, was a fort erected by
The King's retainers, rudely built but strong,
Enribbed with solid bars of ancient oak.
Therein they tarried, save when they went forth
To seek the wild boar in his native haunts,
Or antlered elk, or from the rushing streams
To draw the finny prey.

       The winter now
Began to loose his icy chains, and let
The genial ray enpierce the folding gloom,
Even to the reedy marge of the grey pool
Where in the loneliness the bittern built
Her nest in season, undisturbed of man.
Down in the hollows the brown-fronded ferns
Softly uncurled, but yet the lively shoot
Delayed upon the bough, and all the wood
Still stood unvestured.

      At this time was brought
To the King's camp the tidings of a fight
Waged on the coast of Devon, where the sea
Rolls its grey waves upon the pebbly belt
That zones the fertile vales.   Hubba the Dane
With many a warlike craft did thither come,
But did not thence return, for he and his
Fell fighting by the shore, slain by the men
Of Odune, the brave Devon earl.[10]

        Meanwhile,
Wary and watchful of the chance to strike
Some heavier blow against his enemies,

King Alfred tarried, dwelling in the wilds.
Nor all unfruitful was that quiet life
Of kingly purpose, or of highest act
Of kinghood ; and the thanes that cleaved to him,
Reverenced the more the crownless King, for that
He bore his glory in himself alone.
And much was nobly planned : the prescient thought
Of the great Saxon ruler did shape out
Clearer the form of that which was to be,—
The powerful polity, broad-based on law ;—
The kingdom which should stand, rock-like in strength
Resistive ;—the enfranchised people, great,
And climbing still to greatness !
                                    So the days
Of winter slid into the early spring.

PART II.

THE raven-flag was waving in the wind
Above the tent, where sat the Danish chiefs,
Gothrun and Oskel,[11] with their spearmen bold
Carousing, when a way-worn minstrel came

Beseeching leave to play to them for hire.

"Saxon am I," said he unto the Jarls.

"Once in my country's halls my harp and song

Were welcome, now the minstrel's art is vain,

And as a phantom in a lonely land

I wander aimlessly."   Gothrun the Jarl,

Sat on the high-raised seat, massive of form;

And on the granite of his brow were scars

Of many a fight.   A viking true was he,

With locks loose-flowing like a lion's mane,

Tawny of hue.   In symbol of his rank

Around his mighty-columned throat was wreathed

The golden torque, in long entwisted links.

Turning from him who sat his fellow there,

The aged warrior Oskel, to the bard

Before him, "Sing," he said, "it pleases us.

Set down thine harp, O Angle! Fill yon horn,—

The large one,—thou art welcome; drink, then sing.

Possess ye songs framed in your native speech?"

"Ay, chief: no people under the wide heavens

But have their songs.   Speech hath its roots in song,

And evermore climbs upward into song,
Flowering in golden words." Jarl Oskel said,
" Strike the chords, chant a battle-lay, O scald !"
But Gothrun : " Rather sing to us your gods,
How in the prime of days they made the world,
If handiwork of theirs it be."

                              " One God
We worship, Him who did create of old
The earth and starry heavens.   Listen a song
Of Cadmon,[12] our sweet singer, he who first
Of Saxons sung, how to the harps of God
This goodly structure of the universe
Came forth of chaos.   When th' immortal King
Surveyed the void, where sun nor star was not,
Nor blade of living green, then bade He rise
This ordered world with all its beauteous forms.
Six days the creatorial word went forth,
Till earth, en-wombed in darkness at the first,
Emerged, and canopied with radiant heavens,
Stood with its complete tribes, and set thereon
The crown of creatures—man, in lineaments ·
Divinely fair, wearing the print of God !

                         c

Thou mad'st the sun, Creator Infinite,
And Thou the lily and the rose ! Yea all
Is Thine ; completed thought of Thine own mind,
Not piece-meal, but a living unity,
Work of one will ! "
                              Then interrupting him,
The Danes said, " Ay ; so you may say, but we
Not so believe.   The Æsir made the world,
Our gods : three were they, Odin, Vili, Ve.
They slew the giant Ymir, he who dwelt
In the frost-realms, and of his bones they made
All things that be.   The hills, the ribs of rocks,
The stones and pebbles.   His great skull did frame
The over-arching skies, his brains the clouds,
And of the temples of the mighty head,
The skilful gods fashioned a dwelling place,
Suited for men, Mid-gard, they named it."
                              " Whence came ? "
The Saxon asked, "Whence do ye say he came,
Your giant Ymir ? " One of the great Jarls
Made answer, " Harper, our old sagas teach,
That ages long ago, periods of time

Beyond all count, matter existed, crude,
Unshapen, and the giants of fire and frost,
Coëval lived, and strove together, fierce,
Anarchic, till the man-like god arose,
Our Odin, he who with his brethren joined
Fashioned the world as now we see it.   The three,
The sons of Bor, with cunning fingers carved
Of an ash branch a human pair, the first,
And gave to them life, reason, speech ; our tale
Seems good to us, each people to its faith,
Yours doubtless seemeth good to you.   Go on,
Let us hear more."

                    Commanded thus, he touched
The strings, and gave the sequel of the song
Loved of the Saxons.   And the minstrel sang
Of that fair garden planted of high God
Eastward in Eden, in whose bowers
They dwelt, who were the first of human-kind.
And of the sovereign tree set in the midst,
Bearing the fruit of life, and that near by
Mysterious and forbid their use, but they,
Beguiled by fraud, transgressed His sole command,

Who freely gave Nature's large bounty else.
Thus sinned, and sinning brought death and all ills
Upon their race; and so the wondrous dust,
Built into likeness of the Deity,
Became as other dust, and like to it,
Touched of the finger of corruption.   Hail
To thee Restorer, Thou the promised One,
The woman's seed, who shalt arise to bruise
The Destroyer !"
                    Then said Gothrun : "Stay, O scald,
Stay in your song a little, tell me this,—
Have you not a god who died and rose again ?
We too have our dead god,[13] hymned by our scalds,—
Who shall arise hereafter from deep hell,
Grand as the sun in the Norwegian heavens,
Stupendous, huge, with coronal of flame
Ascending, after the long half-year night
Of winter.   Say, can your god equal ours ;
Can ye tell of an ascension so sublime ? "

" Were it the truth, it were indeed sublime,
But do you count it true, O noble Dane,

For who amongst your people hath beheld
Baldur, the son of light?"
                              Thereat a roar
Of voices rose, " Thor, Thor ! Baldur and Thor !
No gods like ours ! He hath traduced our gods ! "
But Gothrun saying, " Peace ; I bade him speak
Freely," stilled them, and the wild tumult ceased,
But with hoarse mutterings as the vexed sea
Chafes in her surges after tempest passed.

Again the viking questioned : " Know you aught
As grand as that uprising of our god,
Baldur the sun-browed, from th' abodes of death ? "
" Ay, chief : for that sublimity of life
The Christian peoples hold in reverence,
Is a proved verity.   Our Holy One
Hath walked with men on earth, in sight of men
Died, and thereafter rose from out the tomb,
And in the sight of men ascended Heaven,
His throne of glory."
                              The Jarl shook his head.
" We think you fable : what did he, your god ?

Was He strong in battle, was His raised right arm
Invincible to slay His enemies?"
"Not so! He healed the sick and raised the
      dead,
And taught men wisdom, for He came to help,
Not to destroy.   He did the things that one,
A God, who was creator of the world
And loved it, coming into it would do,—
Works of beneficence."

                        Gothrun spoke not,
But drawing lower o'er the deep-set eyes
The wrinkles of his heavy brows, he leant
Upon the carven arm of the great chair
Whereon he sat.   "O scald," he said, at length,
"Magnificent in strength is our great Thor,
Whose mace doth rive the northern hills
To their foundations, loaden with their pines;
But ye account your mightiest to be great,
Simply because He loved, and did men good.
Perchance ye reason justly, but to us
It seemeth strange.   Enough; tarry, O scald,
I will reward thy pains; thou playest well.

Thou shalt sing to me when I am in mood
A war-song of thy people's.

                    Set thine harp
Aside, go find thyself a couch and sleep,
At leisure I will further talk with thee
O minstrel of the Angles ! " Turning then,
Addressed his captains : " See the watch be set,
And bid three hundred of my stoutest spears
Be ready by the dawn to ride with me
On foray.   Soldiers, to a soldier's rest !
Bid that the bugles sound at break of day."
So spake the chief, and rising passed within
The inner tent, and silence presently
Fell on the camp.

                    And so it came to pass,
The Saxon minstrel tarried with the Danes,
Of them made welcome : unrestrained he moved
At will amongst them, looked with curious eyes
Upon their ways, questioned of many things,
And when Jarl Gothrun and his men were pleased,
Sang to them as they sat at feast.   The space
Of seven days he stayed, then prayed, " O chief,

Now let me take my harp and go my way."
But Gothrun : " Wherefore wilt thou go ? remain.
We have lately lost our scald, a goodly one,
Excellent sooth to troll a wassail song,
Or chant a lay to fire the blood i' the veins,
When the war-barques lock on the rolling wave.
Thou art not such as he, but good ; remain."
" No," said the minstrel, " no, it may not be,"—
They were alone, Gothrun and he—" Nay chief,
Seek not to hinder me : perchance my heart
Is heavy for my country's woes.   O Jarl,
I have beheld the peasants' cot, at morn,
Embowered with vines, amid the harvest fields ;
Have passed at eventide, and seen it lie
A heap of smouldering ruins, with charred ribs
Of rafters blackening 'gainst the deep blue sky.
The hapless peasant slain at his own gates,
All beaten into bloody pulp ; have seen
The mother lying dead beside the way,
Her living infant clinging to her breast,
Dappling its innocent hands with blood.   Such sights
Have seared themselves into my brain, and oft

A passion of great sorrow sways my soul,
Like a tempestuous wind, that all night long,
In some lone wood doth bend the trees one way.
I asked of thee for bread, thou gavest it   .
With open hand ; so far my thanks."

                                        " O bard,"
Said Gothrun, " minstrel, I at least know thou,
War not with babes and women !   Go thy way,
Thine heart is not with us, but stay this night
And sing once more a song which pleased me well,
The Phœnix." [14]

                        So the minstrel sang to them
How the majestic bird, sole of its kind
In all the universe, the native birth
Of deserts vast of ancient Araby,
Soared in grand flight, lived out its century life,
Then died, in nest of spicery, self-fired.
Yet ever from the fragrant flame arose,
New plumed, and glorious, with enormous wing
Winnowing the blue sublime.

                                And they were please
Who heard, and with the haft struck on the board

In witness of their praise.

                        It fell by chance
After the banquet of that night, the Dane,
Gothrun, unrestful for the evil dreams
That troubled him, arose, and going forth
In the grey dawn before the camp awoke,
Passed where the bard reposed beside his harp.
The pensive lustre of the early light
Fell on the sleeper's brow, where clustered thick
Soft rings of curls, as on the hyacinth
Cluster the heavy buds. The viking marked
The mighty-moulded chest, bare of the robe
Which, loosened, flowed aside, the puissant arms
On which the curvèd muscle rose, the throat's
Graceful yet massive column : and thus paused
A moment. " He is grand of face, but sad ;
There's sleep upon the eyelids, but the hands
Are as a hunter's in the chase, or like
A warrior's in the fight, when the strong clutch
Is on the falchion. Now he stirs himself,—
He's murmuring—what is it he says ? Ha ! 'Out,
Out Angles !' Dreams he then of fighting ? the gods

O' thy people meant thee for a fighter, man,
And not the jingler of a thing of strings !
No grander warrior truly in my ranks
Had he been bred to arms.   He would not take
The gold I proffered him, but put it by ;
The man is great of soul."   Thus mused the Jarl.

And when the sun was risen on the earth,
Though yet the dewy lids of sleepy flowers
Were weighed with orient drops, the minstrel rose,
And taking up his harp departed thence,
And they of Northland saw him not again.

＊　　＊　　＊　　＊　　＊

Upon the borders of the forest, where
A fountain threw its crystal jets aloft,
Sprinkling with myriad drops the foliage massed
Around its mossy marge, Ethelnoth met
The King returned.   " Dear prince, I did not think
To see thy face again."   And Alfred laughed
A merry laugh thereat.   " Didst thou suppose
That Gothrun had us fast within his toils,
Because we tarried ?   Oh, not so, we light

Upon our feet, you see.   We're safe and sound."
Then by the fountain in the forest spake
King Alfred to his servant Ethelnoth :
" I needs must plough to the rough furrow's end,
Ay, though it lead even to hell's own mouth !
Earl, I will go against the heathen now
To battle, howsoever terrible
The odds."   And Ethelnoth made answer :   " Sire,
Do as thou wilt.   The sublime acts of men
Are touched with foolishness, but haply 'tis
A folly wiser than the wisdom of
The prudent.   As thou purposest so do."

The lady Alswith dwelt in Athelney,
Sharing the toils and lowlihood of life
Of him she loved.   In beauty like a queen,
Though unadorned, she moved, and pleasing showed,
In that antique simplicity ;   more fair,
Beyond her graceful wont, though ever fair.
She came with gladness, in the first of days,
When the green leaf puts forth, and in the groves
The ring-dove's voice is heard ;   hailed of the king,

And of his thanes with gladness, so abode
Within the lonely islet of the woods,
With her the Etheling, and the royal child,
Thereafter lady of the Mercians,[18] who
As such did kindle a proud light of fame,
And left a name, to live amongst the names
Of noble female rulers.

                    One sweet eve
Alswitha said to Alfred as they walked
Amid the bosky glades, " The noble soul
Suffering, makes noble and most beautiful,
Labour, grief, pain, and in its meekness has
A power divine, to turn the things of shame
To ministers of glory. You have done it,
And the lives of all men, learning this, shall be
Made richer and more beautiful thereby."
And Alfred answered her : " Thy words are true,
O sweet my Queen, albeit not true of me.
The lofty spirit sublimates grief, pain,
And is by these itself sublimed ; even so
The divine sonship did fulfil itself
Under obedience, and through grief, toil, pain,

Yea utter shame, acquired its perfectness;
Highest of human lives."

                              Through dim arcades
Of forest trees they wandered, side by side.
The tender buds were greatening on the boughs,
And here and there the pale gold primrose peeped
Or violet, half hidden in the grass,
Known by its scent the most.   In sunny spots
Th' anemonè appeared, or blue-bell raised
The slender stalk, with thickly clustered flowers.
And as they went they lingered oft to mark
The floral growth beside the way, and how
The fern, most delicate of things that God
Created delicate for beauty, spread
The graceful fan luxuriantly.   Anon
They sate them down upon a mossy stone,
Beside a little rivulet that glid,
With soft slow pace, between the nodding sprays
Of drooping willow.   "List," Alswitha said,
"Hark to the lovely warbling of the thrush,
In yonder copse of hazels; how the notes
Rise swelling on the ear, gladsome and sweet;

ATHELNEY.

Thou knowest how we used to love it when
We wandered in the fields about our home
At Chippenham, then most when the white thorn
Came into blossom, and the winds of May
Impregned with fragrance.   Often did we pause
To listen, charmed with the melodious notes,
At twilight, as we strayed along the banks,
Where the full Avon with his azure holds
A mirror to the woody fringe that hangs
Above his borders."

                From the brooklet's side
Through the green solitudes they wended back ;
Yet paused a little on an upland's crest,
Where the thick curtain of the forest fell
Apart, and opened to a clearer view,
There stayed their steps awhile, for now the sun,
Declined to the horizon's rim, shot forth
His fulgent rays, and lit the cloudy range
Of all the west with gorgeous splendour, stretched
Like some vast Pyrenees, whose masses heaped
Pile upon pile, tower up aloft their crags,
And from their broken and indented sides

Cast light and shade, the great dark frame of clouds
Appeared all-glorious, offering to the eye
Its varied vivid hues, and shapes immense,
Here silvered as with snow, there crimsoned deep,
Or dark with heavy purple, a vast scene
Of mingled parts, majestically spread
In mighty scope, and melting gradually
Into the far obscure of haze-like sky,
Which as a sea of faint pale emerald flowed
Immeasurable.

     The lady Alswith said,
When at their lowly cottage door they stood,
" The ripeness of the time is come ; go forth
To battle, and the God of battles make
Thine arms triumphant ! " Then hand within hand,
Beneath the honeysuckle's bloomy sprays,
Between whose fragrant antlers the wild bees
Went in and out, sucking deliciousness,
They passed, silently, through the rustic porch
Into the low-roofed house.

       Then did the king
Lead up his followers from their secret hold,

Through the dim forest paths, where the green earth
Was flashing into flowers, to Egbert's stone,
In Selwood, and set up his standard there,
Sounding the trump of war; and at its voice
Many from out of Wilts and Somerset
Assembled armed, thence undelaying passed
The King and his, to Ethandune, where lay
The army of the North, posted in strength
Upon the pine-clad heights.   Within the vale,
At base thereof, Alfred at night-fall camped,
With purpose to assail the enemy,
And from his seated hold dislodge him.   Few,
Compared with the great host which stood opposed,
Were they with Alfred, but their hearts were true,
And with his handful of brave men, the King
Did set his face to meet the Northern chiefs
With all their strength.

                When in the shadowy east
The first faint lines of light enlaced the clouds
With silver, the great horns, hoarse-voiced and deep,
Sounded the call to arms, and all the camp
Straightway was roused.   The golden blazonry

D

Of the great dragon-standard of the King,
Lifted on high, streamed meteor-like i' the air
Waving, while under ealdorman and thane,
The men of Wessex gathered in their ranks,
Marshalled in order.   Then while the low sun
Begun to kindle in the misty east,
Rising above the shoulders of the hills,
Dark with their crest of pines, the sovereign Voice,
That led the arms of England gave command,
" Up and assail yon heathen host, that now
Haughty in pride doth hold th' adjacent heights,
Defying us ! "

     .   But ere the soldiery,
Obedient to their kingly leader's word,
Formed into line of march, one of his thanes,
Standing by Alfred, lifting up his gaze,
Saw stretched athwart the deep auroral blue
A mass of clouds, whose mighty outlines limned
In opal tints a stately city, vast,
As 'twere a cluster of great towers of gold
Thronged on a mount, and girdled round with walls
Of perfect chrysolite.   This saw the thane,

And cried, " See yon bright vision in the east,
Like some majestic city which old bards
Did love to sing of!" And Alfred saw it,
And pointed it his captains, saying, "See
Yon splendour!" and the captains of his arms
Saw it and wondered, and the army all
Saw it and wondered.[16]   And a shout arose,
" A sign from heaven ! a potent augury
Of victory to be !"   And as they gazed,
Suddenly glowed the massy pile, a-blaze
About its base as if with liquid gold,
Jasper and amethyst, ruby, turquoise,
Jewels of all hues, then to the sight waxed
Paler, and fell away, and the clear sun
Rose in the sky full day.

                        And Alfred set
His battle in array, and forward moved,
Fronting the foe entrenched upon his hill.
In serried files, with wide-extended wings,
The Danes embattled stood, under their chiefs,
Gothrun and Oskel.   Firm-enlocked and high
Their shield-wall, bristling all along the lines

With pointed lances ; mid-most waved their flag,
Bearing enwrought the emblematic bird
Of Odin, and about it stood their best,
Guarding it.   Then, the while the stormful blast
Of martial music rose from the great pipes
Within the midst, the Saxon led his men
In sharpened phalanx forward in swift march,
And charged on the uplifted Danish shields,
Striving to sunder them, and cleave a way
Through that thick front of battle, but in vain,
For as a wall of granite rock they stood,
These of the North.   Again did Alfred form
His shattered column, nor delayed, and now
Charging they burst the shield-wall, and poured in
Between th' opposing spears.

      And with fierce cries
The battle roll'd along the hill, and surged
About its shaggy base, now here, now there.
The falchion smote on targe and helmèd head,
And hurled with mightful hand, the war-axe gleamed,
Whirled swiftly through the air.   Direful the strife ;
Prolonged all day, but Alfred at the last

Stood victor of the field, and looking o'er
Th' ensanguined vale, thick with its heaps of slain,
He saw no man opposing, but far off
The broken foe, fleeing toward his fort ;
While all the way was strewn with shivered arms,
Cast in wild flight ; and fallen in a heap,
The horse and rider lay, pierced by the shaft
Of the pursuer ere the hold was reached
Wherein the remnant of the vanquished Danes
Sought them a shelter.

      Then descended night
With starry silences upon the world
And folding wings of quiet, and the noise
Of battle died away.

    Unto the King
Spake the stout thanes of Wilts and Somerset :
" Now know we thee, victor and lord, sole king,
Who did not doubt before, thee lord and king,
Sole helper ; since before thy sword have fled
These, like the withered leaves before the wind,
When with his shears he cuts the forest locks
In wrathful mood ! "

                              Then sent the Danish chiefs
After the day of battle to the King
To sue for peace, which he accorded them,
Now suppliant to his mercy, urging not
A conqueror's right, but claimed alone of them
The rendering of homage as his fiefs,
And the acceptance of the Christian faith
And of its sacred rites.

                    So at his feet
The heathen lay subdued, and all the land
Resounded with the gentle pipes of peace,
As from the camp at Ethandune, the king
Went up to take once more the regal seat
Of the old kings of Saxony.

                              Then sang
The spinning maidens, sitting at the wheel,
And in the orchards the young children played,
Knowing no fear. Beneath his blossoming vines,
The husbandman sat at the fall of eve
And with his neighbour talked.

                              Learning relumed
Her sacred light within her ancient schools,[17]

And the fair arts entwined their gracious gifts,
And made symmetrical the social life,
Which, now the heads of riot were brought low,
Moved in accord to music of high law,
In stately order and befitting course.

PART III.

ALFRED held court at Wedmore, and with him
Were the great ealdors of the land, his thanes
And ministers, who shared with him the weight
Of government, the pillars of his power.
Thither to the great Witan was to come
Upon the morrow, Gothrun the Danish Jarl,
And his chief captains, to declare themselves
Heathen no more, taking the solemn oaths
Of fealty to the King their over-lord,
Alfred of England,[18] who now stretched the rod
Over her four-fold princedoms.

                           When the pure
Clear pearl of dawning took on it, its first
Of crimson, flushing through the lucid depths

With rose-ensanguined light, the voice o' the trumps
From the great towers proclaimed th' auspicious day,
That was to crown the covenants of peace
With fair accomplishment.   And Alfred passed
Attended by his train, to the high place
Of council, where the assembled senate sate
Awaiting him.   A fillet of pure gold
About the brow expressed him king, nor less
The mantle of imperial purple dye,
Which from the shoulders broad flowed down as low
As to the foot ; and thither came to him
Gothrun and Oskel, and the men of war,
Their captains, and they did him homage.   "Sire,
Bretwalda, we as princes under thee
Henceforth abide, under what yoke of law
Thou puttest on us."   "Rise," said Alfred, "Danes,
No longer foemen.   Say, do you renounce
The Æsir, vainly named as deities,
To worship the one God, sole in the heavens,
Sole in the earth ? "   And Gothrun answered :   " Yea,
We do, we have out-grown the gods of stone,
We have out-worn the fables of our land,

Or else we look behind the mask of myths,
To find a spirit and an essence, His,
Who made the sun, the moon, the stars."

                                        Then said

Alfred the king : " O chiefs, do you indeed
Accept the lowly and most gentle Christ
For lord and master ?   Have ye learned, O Danes,
To suffer is more glorious than to strive,
And man's true greatness as the Son of Heaven,
Lives in his uttermost obedience ? "   " Ay,"
The viking answered, " even so, O King."

Then the high Sovereign, lord of England, said :
" Behold, we give to you a grant of lands,
Champain, and fertile meadow, and green woods,
Skirted with noble rivers, in the east
Of Britain, there, O Danes, to plant yourselves
In peaceful settlement, beside the Celt
And Angle.   Prosper ye and thrive, build towns,
Make markets, over-bridge the rivers, clear
The forest, and drive out the wolf.   We think
The peace we consummate this day shall live

In its great issues, to the after-times,
Fruitful of good.   Saxon,[19] and Celt, and Dane,
We are the roots whereof perchance shall grow
A mighty people in the future ; one
In worship, laws, and speech ; that on the face
Of things to be shall sovereignly imprint
Their potent seal.   This island of the west,
Laved by the silver seas, shall sit secure
In her own strength, and her majestic voice
Send forth through all the world, if we be true
Unto our destiny.   There shall arise
In the far future, as I think, a state,
A noble common-weal, wealthy and free,
Engrafted into which, Celt, Saxon, Dane,
Shall be as one, and Christian ever, till
The seas shall cease to wash these rocky shores,
Or o'er our hills the free breath of the heavens
Blow in reviving gales."

                              So spake the King,
And ceasing, from the daïs where he sate
Descended, and again the trumpets blew
In signal of rejoicing, as they passed

Toward the banquet hall.   With summer flowers
And leafy branches of the forest, elm
. And beech and silver-shining birch, were all
The carven pillars through its spacious breadth
Engarlanded, whilst the clear harp and lute
Gave festal music, soft as when the wind
Breathes amongst flowers, over some rosy bed
Fluting melodiously.   Through the high gates
Enriched with sculptured ornament they passed,
Not without pomp, into the lofty hall
Where was prepared the feast.   On the King's brows
Sat gladness, and his thanes rejoiced, nor less
On th' other side the warlike chiefs, who now
Enlinked themselves in amity with them
Of Alfred's household, and beyond those halls,
Where the great thanes made joy about their lord
Reposing from his wars, th' exultant shouts
Of a rejoicing multitude arose,
Making acclaim, in sound like to the roar
Of waters rushing o'er a rocky bed
Impetuously.

      —   And to the banquet came

The queen Alswitha, and as the prime star,
Which rules the night, puts off her cloudy veil,
And walks in beauty through the astral skies,
She in her gracious loveliness appeared,
Showing undimmed the brow of majesty,
Partaker of her royal consort's joy,
Who in her former low estate with him
Had tasted poverty and bitter grief.

The years went by; and Alfred made his own
Grow to him like a vine most fruitful, whilst
The terror of his name fell on his foes,
And made them quail. At his great bidding came
Artist and scholar from beyond the seas,
And over seas went forth his messengers,
To bring the treasures of the distant lands.
The towered citadel arose, and fane
Where men did worship, and the voice of prayer,
At morning and at evening, from pure lips
Went up without cessation. And they wrought,
Who were the craftsmen of the king, in gold
And silver, and with stately ornament

Enriched the Saxon halls : nor any dared
To lay the thievish hand on costly thing,
Or beautiful.   Such perfect equity
Pervaded all the ways, the woman walked
Through the broad road, or forest greenery,
Protected of her innocence alone,
For he who held the sceptre of the realm,
Did sway a righteous sceptre in those days,
And gave the people whom he loved to rest.

Britain in glory of her crescent power
Rejoiced, and on her noble Ruler's head
The blessings of a grateful nation came.

NOTES TO ATHELNEY.

"The grey day
Was near its close, but ere its sun, which then
Wheeled on the lowest pathway of the year
Sank into darkness."

T was at the end of the year 877 or in the
first days of 878, as we learn from the *Sax.
Chron.*, *Ethelwerd Chron.*, and other
sources, that King Alfred was driven from
his kingdom by the irruptions of the Danes,
who came in unprecedented numbers. The Saxons were
completely overpowered ; the *Sax. Chron.* says the King
escaped with difficulty to the fastnesses of the moors.

" In the year of our Lord's Incarnation 878, which was
the thirtieth of King Alfred's life, the army above-
mentioned went to Chippenham, a royal vill situated in
the west of Wiltshire, and on the eastern bank of the river,
which is called in British the Avon. There they wintered,
and drove many of the inhabitants of that country beyond
the sea by the force of their arms, and by want of the

necessaries of life. They reduced almost entirely to sub-
jection all the people of that country."

ASSER'S *Life of Alfred.*

NOTE 2, p. 2.

" Reaching e'en to the bridles of the horse
Of vision."

See *Revelation,* chap. xiv., ver. 20.

NOTE 3, p. 2.

" This kingdom which I raised
From out its ruins, falls this hour again
To ruin."

Alfred began his reign some seven years previously, at
a period of great trouble and perplexity. By his warlike
energy and enlightened policy he had done much to
restore the kingdom and promote the prosperity of the
people, when the overwhelming attack of his foes frus-
trated his purposes and rendered them abortive. The
Saxons appear to have been greatly discouraged, weary
perhaps of continuing a struggle with an enemy who,
beaten in one place, was sure to presently re-appear in
another, with replenished arms and renewed multitudes.
Asser says, " If thousands of them were slain in one battle,
others took their places to double their numbers."

NOTE 4, p. 3.

" His servant Ethelnoth."

Ethelnoth the Ealdor,—or to use our modern term,
Earl—of Somerset. The old authorities make honourable
mention of his fidelity to the King in the time of his
trouble.

NOTE 5, p. 4.

"Ah, noble thanes,
Think of that field of Ashdune."

The Christians obtained a signal victory over the
Pagans, after a hard-fought contest on the field of
Ashdune or Ashdown, a few years before. The account
of it as found in Asser is interesting. I subjoin an
extract :—

"But here I must inform those who are ignorant of the
fact, that the field of battle was not equally advantageous
to both parties. . . . There was also a single thorn-tree,
of stunted growth, but we have ourselves never seen it.
Around this tree the opposing armies came together with
loud shouts from all sides, the one party to pursue their
wicked course, the other to fight for their lives, their
dearest ties, and their country. And when both armies
had fought long and bravely, at last the Pagans, by the
Divine judgment, were no longer able to beaᵗ the attacks
of the Christians, and having lost great part of their
army, took to a disgraceful flight. One of their two kings,
and five earls were there slain, together with many thou-
sand pagans, who fell on all sides, covering with their
bodies the whole plain of Ashdune."

NOTE 6, p. 5.

"Know I have seen him throned within this hall,
Delivering his judgments to his poor."

It was the custom of the Saxon kings to personally
administer justice. Asser speaks of the great wisdom and
patience of Alfred in inquiring into complicated cases.

NOTE 7, p. 5.

"The two fair children of Alswitha."

The Princess Ethelfleda and Edward the Etheling, King Alfred's eldest children, then of course in their very early years.

NOTE 8, p. 12.

"The woodman's wife looked on him as her thrall."

The story of the cakes is too well known to need to be recounted here.

NOTE 9, p. 13.

"On the borders of the isle
Of Athelney."

Probably on the spot where the piety of the King afterwards caused a monastery to be erected. See Asser's *Life of Alfred.*

NOTE 10, p. 14.

"slain by the men
Of Odune, the brave Devon earl."

This was the battle fought at Kenwith Castle, near Westward Ho! the site of which tradition still points out.

NOTE 11, p. 15.

"The Danish chiefs
Gothrun and Oskel."

Two of the Jarls who led the army invading the provinces of the West Saxons. Gothrun is styled the "King of the Pagans," he was probably the chief leader.

NOTE 12, p. 17.
" Listen a song
Of Cadmon, our sweet singer."

Cadmon was a friend of the pious Abbess Hilda, and sung the story of the Creation in Saxon verse at her request. See Bede's *Eccl. Hist.*

NOTE 13, p. 20.
" We too have our dead god."

The death of Baldur was a favourite theme of northern poetry.

NOTE 14, p. 25.
" a song which pleased me well,
The Phœnix."

The Saxons were very fond of this legend of the East, it is found in many of their poems yet existing. They appear to have considered it an emblem of the Resurrection.

NOTE 15, p. 29.
" The royal child,
Thereafter lady of the Mercians."

Ethelfleda, Alfred's warlike daughter, is a very noble figure in early English history. See *Florence of Worcester* and *Saxon Chron.* for particulars respecting her.

NOTE 16, p. 35.
" A sign from heaven ! a potent augury
Of victory to be ! "

The Saxons were wont to view all remarkable appearances in the heavens with superstitious regard.

NOTE 17, p. 38.

"Learning relumed
Her sacred light within her ancient schools."

Alfred did much to encourage learning, notably at Oxford and Winchester.

NOTE 18, p. 39.

"Alfred of England."

Although he never styled himself King of England, Alfred was to all intents such, the divisions of the heptarchy being now obliterated. The princes of Northumbria, Mercia, and Anglia having been either slain or driven into exile by the Danes, the rule of the whole country lay in Alfred's hands.

NOTE 19, p. 42.

"Saxon, and Celt, and Dane,
We are the roots whereof perchance shall grow,
A mighty people in the future."

It is not impossible of belief that such a glorious forecast of the future should occur to the mind of the great Saxon Prince. We know that Alfred did much to promote a general amity, and to establish a common Christianity in the land. He showed great favour to his British subjects and was greatly beloved of them. The Celtish princes of Demetia voluntarily sought his friendship and powerful protection. His generosity to the Danes in many instances is very marked, notably so in the case of Hastings, whose sons he returned to him, enemy though he was, ransomless and free, because they had been baptised. We may trace in this not only the

chivalrous and romantic generosity of a noble-minded
prince, but also the policy of the far-seeing ruler who
sought to bridge over the old animosities of race ; and to
convert enemies into friends and allies,—foes into peace-
ful subjects and law-abiding citizens. It is remarkable
that it is to a Briton, namely Asser (appointed by Alfred
to the bishopric of Crediton,—or Exeter,—after he came
at the King's desire from St. David's in Wales), we are
indebted for the fullest record we possess of the life and
deeds of the greatest of the Saxon kings.

EASTER DAY.

ISE, gentle morn, and shed thy beams,
Red from the rosiest heart of dawn,
In sign of that great life divine,
From which our holiest hopes are drawn !
Spread out, oh ! rose of light
Your leaves, to glad our sight,
Symbol of that more bright
Which blossom'd from the tomb !

Lo now the beautiful feet of Spring,
That dapple the green earth with flowers,
Come softly, and behind them leave
Touches of gold in woody bowers,

In fields, and meads, and groves,
The which to haunt she loves.
Young buds where'er she moves
Tell out that she has come,

  The beautiful daughter of the year,
To quicken to new life the earth.
  In rippling brooklets crisp and clear,
The low glad laughter of her mirth
      Tinkles, where wild birds sing,
      Or dip the stream with wing,
      For now in everything
      Subtilly soft and fine,

  Beauty and music wake and live.
Oh, beautiful feet, upon the hills,
  Eastward, where kindles the great sun !
Oh, beautiful feet, beside the rills
      Where the young leaflets quiver !
      Nature thou tellest ever,
      Stammering and pausing never,
      Of that great life divine,

Which blossomed from the darksome grave,
First-fruits of glorious life to be,
  When Christ arose, and gave to men
The pledge of immortality !
      For each new morn doth show,
      With its red clouds a-glow,
      Each Spring when violets blow,
      As in a mystery,

  In the sweet light conquering the dark,
In the sweet life new won from death,
  In heaven's wide arc of blue above,
In all earth's greenery beneath,
      Shadowings of that great glory
      Told in the sacred story.
      Oh, breast of earth so flowery,
      Thou tellest it for aye,

  As with a thousand lips to men,
The rising of the blessed one,
  The triumph of the Son of God,
Who vanquished death, and dying won

A deathless life for all !
O thou with seed-pearls small
That on the grasses fall,
Come on thy golden way !

Come, gentle morn, and shed thy beams,
Bring forth the ruby of the dawn,
 In sign of that great life divine,
From which our holiest hopes are drawn !
    Spread out, oh rose of light,
    Your leaves, to glad our sight,
    Symbol of that more bright   .
    Which blossom'd from the tomb !

GARFIELD.[1]

UMANITY that keeps her best
    As jewels in her heart,
    Shall give him loving place therein,
  The man who with sweet art,
In all the devious walks of life,
  Combined high thought with deed,
Making the common drudgeries move
  To music that doth feed
The ideal springs of love, and still
  As soldier, statesman, friend,

[1] It was asked by the dying President of one attending him,
' Do you think I shall have a place in history?" "Yes," it was
eplied, " a high place, and a grand place in the human heart."

In camp, and senate, and in home,
  Was stedfast to one end !

While this old Saxon stock puts forth
  Its blossoms to the light,
Rose-like, beyond the western seas,
  His memory shall be bright ;
And wheresoe'er this speech of ours,
  In far-off future days,
Shall sound beneath th' encircling skies,
  The tale of him shall raise
Heroic fire in noble hearts,
  And men shall fondly say
The lustre of a name like his
  Shall never pass away !

The patriot sows the lowly seed
  Which germinates in power ;
Upon the basis of pure lives
  Great nations rise and tower ;
The good, the pure are they that make
  Those deep foundations strong

Whereon the State securely rests ;
  Nor loftier theme of song
With trumpet-blowings rings through time
  Than the just deeds of one
Who sets his country's good above
  All interests of his own !

Oh great star-banner of the States
  Wave gently o'er the dead !
We give the tribute of our tears ;
  A mighty people's head,—
A little less than king, and more,—
  Is now this day laid low !
And in our island home we feel
  The touch of that great woe
Which thrills the myriads of yon realm.
  A strain of something grand
Is in such sorrow, and it strikes
  A chord within this land !

Oh great star-banner of the States,
  Float proudly in the wind !

Sons of the great and free march on,
    Lead in the march of mind !
Strike down foul tyranny and wrong,
    Exalt true liberty !
In vanguard of the nations move,
    The world's true chivalry !
Open the golden doors of Peace,
    Prepare the glorious way,
The future pathway of mankind
    Unto the peerless day !

LINES ON THE DEATH OF
THE PRINCESS ALICE.

H ! emerald leaf upon the summer bough,
The dreary rains shall weep on thee, for thou
Shalt fade and fall !

Oh ! ruby-hearted rose of golden June,
Queenliest of flowers, thou, too, shalt droop full
soon,
And fade and fall !

She, too, hath faded, England's treasured flower,
Most perfect daughter proved in the dark hour,
Alas ! her fall !

Faded, our sweetest rose, ah ! woe the day,
That one so fair, so dear, should pass away—
                    Should fade and fall !

Cold, cold ! no smile, no kiss ! oh, husband, weep !
Weep, oh, young babes ! alas ! for that strange sleep !
                    To fade and fall

In her best bloom, mother and wife, too sad !
Yet the sweet Heaven its part in her hath had !
                    Why weep her fall ?

But we ? Ah ! our poor hearts ache in the dark,
Hungering in vain, we see not God's high mark.
                    Oh ! weep her fall

Ye four-fold millions of our Nation's heart,
All England had in her some noble part,
                    Weep, weep, her fall !

Grieve, England, for the daughter of our Queen,
Loved with full love as she hath ever been.
                    We fade and fall

As doth the leaf, alike the high, the low
Oh ! mighty lesson of a mighty woe !
            We fade and fall !

THE OLD YEAR AND THE NEW.

 SAID to the departing Year,
   " Tarry a little, I have within my mind
   A dream of a god of the mythic times,
Let me carve it a statue ere you go, and bind
  The unseen with the seen."
 But the year made answer unto me,
   " Too late, too late ! "

 Then said I to the passing year,
" Oh stay a little, I have within my hand
 A lot of seed-pearls, let me string them up,
Lest they be scattered in a lonely land
  Where they'll be lost I ween."

But the year made answer unto me,
     " Too late, too late ! "

And again I said unto the year
" Oh tarry, tarry, there is within my heart
    A love that has not yet been told
To one who pines for it.   Do not depart
      Till I have told my love."
    But the year made answer unto me,
      " Too late, too late ! "

    Then said I to the passing year,
" Tarry, oh tarry yet ; I heard just now
    The cry of a little lamb in the dark,
I was sleepy, I did not stir, but how, ah how !
      If the lamb I love doth rove ? "
    But the year made answer unto me,
      " Too late, too late ! "

    And I wept for the words of the dying year.
I wept, and solemn spirits of the night
    Spake each to other, " Too late, too late ! "
But anon from the east, with the springing light,

F

Came the sound of a still sweet voice,
I cried "What hope?" and it answer'd me,
"Behold, I wait!"

For God had sent His glad New Year;
From the young eyed cherubs that nestle about His feet,
On its errand of gentle love it came.
"What hope?" I cried, then the voice most sweet,
"O soul, up and rejoice,
I come with new light, rise, I await thee,
Behold, I wait!"

LIFE.

WHAT says the spring wind to the rose,
Waking her in the morning? " Life,
oh life,
Oh the glad free life,
'Tis life, and life, and nothing but life ! "

What says the river as it flows,
To the tiny buds a-bursting ? " Life,
Oh the glad free life,
'Tis life, and life, and nothing but life !"

What is it, O lyric lark, you sing
In the ears of morning ? " Life, oh life,
Oh the glad free life,
'Tis life, and life, and nothing but life I"

And in my heart the glad thought lifts the wing
        With each new dawning, Life, oh life,
            Oh the glad free life,
'Tis life, and life, and nothing but life !

But I hear the sound of feet in the street,
        ·They are carrying a child to the grave.   Ah
            death,
            Not life, but death,
Death hath its way, after all is death !

And the living voices that are so sweet
        Die out in the dark night's silence, death,
            Ah me, 'tis death,
Death hath its way, after all is death.

And I sigh within my heart, and weep,
        Death is twin of life, its equal is death,
            Its stronger is death,
Death hath its way, after all is death !

Is it so ? I know not ; a voice from the deep,
        And it moaneth ever, " Death, ah death,

The all-conquering death,
Death hath its way, after all is death ! "

But the higher voice in the brighter hours
Groweth clearer ever, " Life 'tis life,
The victorious life,
' Tis life, and life, and evermore life ! "

Now the wind is playing amongst the flowers
This Easter morning, and it singeth, " Life,
Oh the glad free life,
'Tis life, and life, and evermore life ! "

LINES

SUGGESTED BY THE OPENING OF ROCK
PARK, BARNSTAPLE, 12TH
AUGUST, 1879.

HE vine hath its own glory of the grape,
  The ripen'd wheat the beauty of its
   gold;
Yea, these are excellent; yet more divine,
 In its pure deeds of selfless love unrolled,
  The fruitage of a noble life.

The lowly plant from root and leaf goes up
 Unto the bright consummate flower—its crown;
By steps of faithful love, the loving soul
 Climbs up to that great virtue of its own,
  God-like, with all sweet goodness rife !

The flower, the fruitage of a noble life—
  Yes, we behold it in our midst this day ;
We know and name it ; it is here with us ;
  An excellence which shall not pass away,
      Nor fade nor wither like the leaf !

The world with its brute-lusts shall reel and pass ;
  The things of tinsel melt like mists of morn ;
The base, the mean, die in its littleness ;
  But all that is of selfless goodness born
      Shall be as is the full ripe sheaf !

The false notes die in distance in the hymn ;
  But the true notes live on, and make the song
Sweet to the ears of them that stand afar.
  And all true virtue shall live on, and long,
      Aye ever, be a thing of power !

Oh ! not as rain upon the barren sands,
  Shall loving deeds fall on the hearts of men ;
But fruitful still to bring forth only good,
  Thy gifts shall reach their end, oh ! doubt it not !
      Thou kindly giver at this hour !

Our old town sent him forth, long years ago :
   Needs must it be that she should love him much
Who loves her still so well, who through all change
   Hath loved and served : she hath not many such
      Amongst her sons, so pure, so true !

" Beauty, and good, and knowledge," the sweet three
   Beneath one roof, the better for his care,
Shall thrive and grow, and make this ancient town
   Happy and free : the future years shall bear
      Their tribute to his praise, most due !

A daughter of the town, I give him thanks !
   Ay, for the sake of that old home of mine.
There first with baby hand I plucked the flowers,
   When the glad spring, with tender shower and shine,
      Opened the violet's eyes of blue.

Ay, long my native town shall hold him dear,
   And teach her sons to copy as they may
So fair a course ; to be, like him, just, pure,
   Loving, and true ! " Here," she shall say,
      " Behold the pattern of a life

" Lived out to ends of truest usefulness."
　And haply some of these her sons shall be,
In commerce or in art, leaders of men,
　Teaching the true, giving blind eyes to see,
　　Bidding to cease the world's harsh strife.

THE CUP OF TEARS.

HE child was young and fair,
    Soft its eyes and bright its hair,
    But sickness on it lay,
And the little one passed away ;
The mother she wept in her grief,
Disconsolate without relief,
Day and night wept she,—night and day.
It was midnight, and there rose,
In the chamber small and dim,
Where no fire nor lamp-light glows,
With sound of music mild
The semblance of a child,
A visionary babe—
Lovely angel of the Lord,
Such as those who wait His word,

And soft before him wave
Fragrant censers of their praise,
While a ceaseless song they raise,
Tender looks of love it wore,
In its hand a cup it bore,
Full was it unto the brim,
Filled unto the topmost rim.
The midnight air was riven
With the voice so soft and clear,
Thus it spoke, the vision bright,—
" From the angelic bower,
Where nestling cherubs sleep
Beneath the wings that keep
In shelter close and deep
The little ones of heaven,
In this sweet and solemn hour
Come I to thee, my mother dear.
Lo ! the sorrow-cup I bear,
In it gathered every tear
Weeping thou for me hast shed :
If the cup should overflow,
Though among the saints I glow,

And the heavenly dances tread,
Must I taste of mortal woe,
And in mourning bow me low!"
Thus it spoke, then passed from sight,
The lovely child of light.

And the mother wept no more ;
  Hushed she for her darling's sake
All her grief so great and sore
  Lest the little one partake.

LINES

ON THE OCCASION OF MR. GLADSTONE'S
LATE VISIT TO LEEDS.

VINE amongst the nations on whose
  boughs
 Truth, justice, peace do hang like golden
   fruit,
Our England—lo, great souls and pure do feed
 Thy secret strength, thou of the mighty root !
Amongst the nobler sons of England, one
 Stands foremost at this moment—a great name
Amongst the names that have their lustre won
 By years of faithful service ;—his the aim
No mean ambition sullies, his the life
 Harmonious with the principles of love,

The nature " finely moved to issues fine,"
  Should we not love him well, whose worth we prove

A noble statesman, he has done good work,
  For he has helped to break the oppressive yoke,
To set to healthful music all the steps
  Of social life, to ward the bitter stroke
Of grinding misery from defenceless heads,
  To make men men, knowing their heritage !
Not shifting with the veering times, but still
  The people's friend, though factions idly rage.
His the clear word, and his the guiding hand,
  All honour to the aged statesman be,
Still he is strong to hold the reins of power,
  And grandly lead a nation of the free !

The thought of half the spacious globe to-day
  Is moulded in this Saxon speech, the tongue
Which Shakespeare used shall give new wings of wor
  To many a future poet's song,
And Saxon laws shall set their sovereign stamp
  On institutions of the times to be.

Justice, and truth, and peace are yours to guard,

  O England's sons ! the glorious and the free !

Yea, let the great tree flourish in far days,

  Amongst the tribes of earth, the pure, the just.

Hang on her boughs like golden fruit, O sons,

  Till the vine trail her blossoms in the dust !

October, 1881.

THE LONG AGO.

N a green and pleasant garden
    There was once a fairy bower;
    It was built to sound of harps
In a soft and golden hour,
    Long ago, and long ago!

Thither came the fays and sylvans,
    Tripping lightly with sweet songs,
And the zephyrs in the groves
    Answered them with airy tongues,
    Long ago, and long ago!

Linkèd with a chain of roses,
    Thither came the Graces three,

And the laughing son of Venus,
  Cupid with his archery,
    Long ago, and long ago!

To that arbour, flower-embosomed,
  Came the rosy-wingèd Hour
That unlocks the gates of day,—
  Laid him down within the bower,—
    Long ago, and long ago!

And the sylvans of the garden
  Spake unto the lovely guest,
" Tell us, O most gentle sprite,
  Art thou come with us to rest?"
    Ah me, 'twas long ago!

To the sylvans of the garden,
  Answer made the child of light,
" I am come to rest awhile
  In the lily's bosom white."
    Oh, it was long ago!

And the gentle fays and sylvans
  Questioned him—" What dost thou love
Is it music mild and soft,
  Played within a shadowy grove?"
          (Ah it was long ago !)

" While to the soft Lydian measure,
  O'er the daisy-sprinkled ground,
We with dainty feet do dance
  In a circle round and round?"
          Oh, it was long ago !

Then the sound of laughter ringing
  Filled the garden through and through,
For the fays in frolic ran
  Where the fairest flowerets grew,—
          All this was long ago !

And the boughs of Flora stripping,
  Brought by armfuls the ripe flowers,
Singing, " Strew them round and round,

Strew them in bright fragrant showers !"
    Ah, it was long ago !

And the sylvans and the garden,
  And the rosy-wingèd Hour,
Where they are I wot now,
   But the leaden day goes slower
    Than in the long ago !

WITH A WREATH AND CROSS OF WILD FLOWERS SENT TO A BEREAVED FRIEND.

O, little wildling flowers,
    Plucked from the heart of Devon's woods
    Go, touched with tears of ours !
A lowly tribute to his worth,
Who sleeps—Life's task well done !
Ah, gentle buds and sweet,
Emblems of the mind's varying moods ;
Is it not right and meet
That you, the fair earth's loveliest birth
Should for the dead be won ?

Go, in soft ministry,
And what the spoken word still fails

To utter, that speak ye !
Tell our regrets for him, low laid,
And how we loved him say !
Where the wild grasses wave,
Swept by the winds, in our green vales
I pluck'd you.   On yon grave
Lie lightly, till your blossoms fade
And graceful leaves decay.

Brief is this little life
Though " threescore" measure out its span
And still, with troubles rife,
And fragile, are all works of ours,
Evanescent as the dew !
Methinks I learn it now
More deeply than before, how man
Moves in a passing show,
Whether in sunshine or in showers
Brief are his days and few !

And yet a ray divine,
Springs from a life that's nobly lived ;

Subtilly soft and fine,
It kindles and throws out its beams
Along the rolling years !
Oh, like a pearl most white
That's found by one who deep hath div'd,
It hangs in radiance bright
Upon the world's great heart, and seems
Bedewed with tender tears,

To grow more beautiful !
The brother that you mourn, dear friend,
Who was so dutiful
To all the high behests of Heaven,
Leading a life most pure,
Enshrined in our deep love,
Lives still, nor misses one true end
Of that for which he strove.
The beauty of his soul is given
To us, yet more and more,

As death takes off the veil.
Lie lightly on his grave, oh, flowers

Until ye droop and fail !

Touched with the droppings of fresh tears,

Enwreath his place of rest !

Go, in soft ministry,

And what the spoken words of ours

Say not, express !   Ah, me !

Something of pain life ever bears ;

Only the dead are blest !

October, 1882.

A SUMMER SONG.

OW blows the crimson rose, and the sweet
                    white,
          Now lolls the lily on the silver wave,
Now the full-throated thrush sings to delight
    His brooding mate.   The swans their plumage lave,
              Gliding adown
              The azure lake.
Now sweetens in the fruit the tender juice,
    The cherry's ruby clusters ripening glow;
Shakes the laburnum her bright tresses loose,
    While honeysuckles their sweet breathings blow;
              Where shades embrown,
              June's wood flowers wake.

With softest rustlings from the balmy south,
    Young Zephyr comes to fan the dreamy flowers,

Sweeter than sweetest kisses on the mouth ;
 Led in by meek-eyed Morn, with dewy showers
   Dropped on the meads
   Like orient pearls.
Within the woodland's green and dusky glades,
 The running rivulet laughs and brawls, now leaps
And gleams in sunshine, now glooms in the shades ;
 Where the warm sunlight falls subdued and sleeps,
   The fern 'mong weeds
   Lifts its brown curls.

Now in the deep of night, in secret place,
 The nightingale her passionate music pours
On the thrilled air, so hath she only grace
 To sing in silence, and these hearts of ours
   Float into love's
   Own deep divine !
Now, oh dear love of mine, my Psyche sweet,
 With golden zone, gaze in mine eyes with thine,
And let the gorgeous blooms of summer meet
 In our twinned souls, more pure, spiritually fine,
   Than in her groves
   Oh love of mine !

TO A BUTTERFLY.

COME, rest by me,
    With gilded wing upon the flower,
    And charm me for one fleeting hour!
        Come, rest by me,
And make me joyful with the sight
Of an embodied beam of light !
            Dear child of spring !
Sweet April's fairest darling thou,
That gently flutterest round her brow,
            When from her heart
Goes up through leaf and bud above
The first faint thrill of virgin love !

Most beauteous thing
That Nature has, how fair thou art,
And yet of strength how small thy part !
One touch of mine
Would brush the beauty from thy wing,
And unto dust thy glory bring !
Great Nature's child,
Go, sport upon the mother's breast !
But for a moment is thy rest.
I own—I feel
A life whose vast immensity
Ages unroll : and yet there be
Some ties which bind
My soul to thee, thou trembling thing.
And there be thoughts untold that bring—
Tremblingly bring—
The tear-drops to mine eyes : sweet thought
And tender memory are brought
Of days long past :
The joy and sorrow of a dream
With thy bright flickering gleam.

TO A BUTTERFLY.

Creature so frail,
I, that am human, own with thee
Some links of sympathy : to me,
Sweet wanderer,
Thou art no insect, but a light
From out the past, tender and bright !

THE RIVER.

 H, lazy meandering river,
　　　'Tween grassy banks and lolling flowers,
　　　Through all the golden summer hours,
　Flowing on softly ever,
Toward the far-off mighty sea,
What singeth thy low wave to me?

　Though lapped in such sweet feeling,
As folds the odorous heart of flowers,
When fed with rains in July hours,
　Some weirdly strange revealing,
Oft dashes the soul's laughter
With shade of the hereafter!

Our most delicious dreaming—
Though we do couch on honeyed flowers,
While dance around the rose bright hours—
   Is with an innate sorrow teeming,
And from our gleefullest gladness
Start tears with freight of sadness.

Thou flowest on, oh river!
'Tween grassy banks with lolling flowers,
Through all the golden summer hours,
   To fall and be for ever
Enwrapped within the infinite sea—
So pass we on to mystery.

MAY MORNING.

HE darkness is gone,
   The glad lark is singing,
May, leaf-crowned, comes on,
   Her blossoms she's bringing !
      My fairest, arise !

The laughing brooks leap,
   Flashing out to the sun.
Love, wake from thy sleep,
   The day has begun !
      My fairest, arise !

The violets are sweet,
   As they bud in a row—

O turn hither thy feet,
 Where the wild flowrets blow!
  My fairest, arise!

As to kisses of love,
 Earth awaketh this hour,
List the voice of the dove,
 Cooing soft in her bower!
  My fairest, arise!

O come to me, sweet,
 In the arbour of roses,
One kiss as we greet
 All Eden discloses!
  My fairest, arise!

THE COLD GREY SEA.

 COLD grey sea so old,
  What is it thou dost say,
With the lapping of thy waves,
  Upon the pebbles grey ?

Thou hidest in thine heart
  A solemn mystery,
And therefore thou art sad,
  O thou most ancient sea !

Thy grey waves ebb and flow,
  With a monotone of pain,
Like the pain within the soul
  Of one who loves in vain !

H

With mournful murmurings,
   Thou breakest on the shore,
I pace by thee and dream,
   What shall be nevermore !

Ah me ! thou cold grey sea,
   What is it thou dost say,
With the lapping of thy waves,
   Upon the pebbles grey ?

Thou echoest the pain,
   Of this our human heart,
The sorrow and the doubt,
   Wherewith we inly smart !

The pining and regret,
   The longing infinite,
That haunts our whole of life,
   And the hopeless cry for light !

With mournful murmurings,
. Thou breakest on the shore,
I pace by thee and dream
What shall be nevermore !

"THY KING COMETH UNTO THEE, O ZION."

IDE on, ride on, O kingly One !
 We children of to-day,
Will shout hosanna, as they did
Who strewed with palms Thy way !

Not as a conqueror from war,
 In meekness Thou dost come !
Music and song shall welcome Thee,
 Sweet songs from every home !

Ride forth, ride forth anew, O Christ,
 Lord of all times and men !

The day-star of the waiting world,
  As truly now as then !

Thy throne Thou dost up-build, great Lord,
  Within the human soul,
And there, as kingly conqueror,
  Thy banners dost unroll !

Not in dim aisles alone is found,
  A temple meet for thee,
The heart that glows with fervid flame
  A sacred shrine shall be !

In grand apocalypse appear,
  Anew thou heavenly One !
The nations are Thine heritage,
  Thine are they, Thine alone !

Ride forth, O conqueror divine,
  We children of to-day,
Will shout hosanna, as they did
  Who strewed with palms Thy way !

REDEMPTION.

 ISE my soul on wings of faith,
    To the heavenly gates above.
    Sing thou there with clearer voice,
  Of a dying Saviour's love !

There beside the fountain sing,
  Flowing from the emerald throne,
Where the bleeding lamb is found,
  With the wounds that did atone !

High above earth's fleeting things
  Sing redemption's sweetest song,
Sing of Jesu's love to men,
  Than the might of death more strong.

Tell the world the Saviour lives,
　Throned in light for evermore,
And the souls that captive be
　From the dust may upward soar.

They in mire of sin that lie,
　As on wings of doves shall rise,
Hearing the sweet strain of love
　Wafted from the glorious skies !

THE VOICE FROM HEAVEN.

HEN from the radiant cloud of old
    The heavenly dove came forth,
Men list'ning heard the voice of God,
    And knew the Saviour's worth !

A little band, they stood that day,
    By Jordan's deep blue wave,
And looked upon the lowly One,
    Divinely sent to save !

The centuries have rolled their course,
    A thousand years and more,
Yet still to us the message comes
    From Galilee's far shore !

And still from out the covering cloud,
   That veils our highest light,
The bird of God anew comes forth,
   In goodness infinite !

Light in our midst, sweet dove this hour,
   And under brooding wings,
The little ones in grace receive,
   Until the whole land rings,

With glad hosannas meetly raised,
   By childish voices sweet,
Come where the children gather now,
   Their loving Lord to meet.

Come heavenly Dove, from heaven above,
   Come voice that speaks of Him
Who is the whole world's light of life
   Unto its utmost rim !

ELIM.

EXODUS XV., 27.

H for the palms and fountains,
   The shadowy palms that grow,
By Elim's many fountains,
  Whose waters softly flow!

Oh, there they rest from labour,
  And there they chant the psalm,
That soundeth sweet to angels,
  All in a golden calm!

Most dreary is the desert;
  Grant, Lord, a little rest!
I sigh, foot-sore and weary,
  For that green vale so blest!

Be Christ to me as Elim,
  My peace amid the strife,
And be His love my shelter,
  Through all the ills of life !

Within my Saviour's favour
  Fountain and palm I find,
The burning blinding desert,
  Forgotten, lies behind !

I find in Him my gladness,
  My rest and my repose,
When He His face uplifteth
  My soul no sorrow knows !

To Thee, O gentle Saviour !
  Thine own shall still repair,
And resting in Thy presence
  Cast off their grief and care.

FORGIVENESS.

H, come and kiss the bleeding feet,
　　Nailed to the shameful tree !
　Come in your chains of guilt and sin,
　　Come in your misery,
　　　　Come to the feet of Him
　　　　Who died to set you free !

Come, and your hearts of stone shall melt,
　To think such love should be
So long despised, so long denied,—
　Sinner, He cares for thee !
　　　　Come to the feet of Him
　　　　Who died to set you free !

The new pure heart shall Christ bestow,
　Oh, taste His liberty !

Pardon and peace He giveth you,
  His joy your own shall be,
      Come to the feet of Him
      Who died to set you free !

Oh, kiss with tears the bleeding feet
  Nailed to the shameful tree !
Come men, come women, stained with sin,
  Slaves sold to infamy,
      Come to the feet of Him
      Who died to set you free !

IN MEMORIAM.

OLD the meek hands that work no more,
    And o'er them strew the pure white
        flowers!
The angels' eyes may look on her,
  Alas! no longer is she ours,
      Sleep gently, gentle one,
      Thine earthly task well done!

Such beautiful serenity
  In life was hers, we will not weep—
Not wildly; still her spirit holds
  Such power on us, though grief be deep,
      Our hearts are hushed and still,
      Submissive to God's will!

He rounds this little life of ours
  With His own vast eternity,
No broken fragment is it then,
    'Tis but a portion that we see !
        The fulness of our life,
        Lies out beyond earth's strife !

In exquisite completeness now
  He carves a statue of His own,
His fair ideal, out of that
    Which lately we called ours ; alone
        He does it, meaner hand
        Shapes not His type so grand.

Why should we sorrow then ?   Ah why !
  We wait till His revealing hand,
Shall lift the veil, and show the form
    So beautiful, in that fair land
        Where all is peace is joy,
        Where love knows no alloy !

MY SONG.

Y song is like the bird's
 That builds beneath the eaves,
When the winds of spring are soft,
 At the budding of the leaves,
 'Tis fed of love !

To you and me 'tis sweet,
 Who meet and clasp and kiss,
But other souls than ours,
 I ween would haply miss
 The charm we prove,

A lyric of the heart,
 A simple homely strain

That falls upon the ear :
  And comes and comes again,
      All songs above !

To thee, O sweeting, I
  Sing at the break of day,
And when the brown shades fall,
  Whilst with loitering steps we stray
      Through the green groves !

THE LILY OF THE VALE.

 SAW in dreams young cherubs stand
About the feet of God; their wings were
white,
Their wings were bright, and round about them shed
Ambrosial sweets! The heavenly Father spoke
In accents clear and loud; through heaven His voice
Was heard, "Which of my children, pure and white,
Will go for Me to earth? Among my bands
Of radiant saints in this fair Paradise,
Where shall I find my meetest messenger,
To bear to earth, and on her breast diffuse
The fragrance and the purity of this
Mine holy dwelling place?"
                    Then saw I stand.

Before His face, a cherub mild and fair,
More lovely than a child of earth, but like
To such it seemed—a fair and female child.
" Father, I go," she whispering said, then bowed,
And veiled her with her lovely wings, all pure,
And sweet as petals of the lily-flower.
I saw the moving of a thousand wings,
And far and wide the glory-fields of heaven
Were filled with breath of odours rich.

        Such was
My dream ; its meaning then I did not know,
Nor scarcely know I now.

        It was the spring,
The late bare earth was flush with wealth
Of new blown-buds, when in a vale I stood,
And with delicious joy, low at my feet,
Beheld a lily 'mid her clustering leaves,
Seated in queenly grace.   She from the sight
Did half-withhold her beauty, half revealed,
Half hid, amid those green and shining leaves,
Looking on her, I seemed to see again
The vision of my dream ; the face of God.

And the white angel standing at His feet,
And all the fragrance of the heavenly fields
Renewed itself that hour.   I hailed and blessed
The lovely grace, the maiden of my dream,
The incarnate cherub in the flower.

TO THE SNOWDROP.

EFORE the first red buds of spring unfold,
  Or cuckoo's voice is heard, thy face is
      seen,
    Flower of the winter hail !
    Thou wee sweet darling hail !

Sweeter to me than April's opening buds,
Or flowers and scented blossoms of the May,
      Thy snowy spotless white
      And fresh green leaves appear.

The primrose and the violet bloom, in woods
Among their kind, but thou on the bare breast
      Of earth, a single grace,
      When all beside is reft.

κ

Young Flora's messenger before her sent
To herald in her sweet approach ; thou com'st
  A token and a pledge,
  A lowly, meek evangel.

I gaze on thee, and dream the ecstasy
Of spring, the beauty of the spring, whose heart
  Of mystery shall ope
  In buds and blooms and glories.

Thou art to me, sweet flower, a thing of joy,
To me thou art a prophecy of beauty,
  For ever beautiful,
  For evermore a joy.

A snowdrop amid winter's snow, I too
Would bloom like thee in spotless purity :
  Like thee would prophesy
  Of sweetness yet to come.

THE THROSTLE.

HE throstle singeth to his mate,
Within the green-wood tree,
Merrily, oh merrily—
Where the wild breeze bloweth free,
Ah, heart of mine,
What singeth he?

Perched lightly on the leafy bough,
He trills his gentle lay,
While the dewdrop lies within the flower,
Just opening to the day,
From whose chalice fine,
Sips the wild bee!

" Oh the world is ever young," singeth he,
   " Ever new are life and love,
Ever sweet, ever young"—so the carol flows—
   And the branches sway above,
      In their lively green,
      By the spring new-dressed !

" Oh, life is a goodly thing," sings he,
   " And joy is its perfect crown."
And he flitteth away to the far-off fields,
   Returning anon to his own,
      When the sun is seen
      In the rosy west.

The throstle singeth to his mate,
   Within the green-wood tree,
Merrily, oh merrily,
   Where the wild breeze bloweth free,
      O heart of mine,
      Thus singeth he !

TO W. F. R.

ROM our loved Devon do I send
These winter flowers with greetings due,
On this his natal day,
To him who loves our Devon well,
And of her flowers has often sung
In many a charming lay !
Around these snowdrops I would twine
Some simple lines to say how true
The wishes that are ours,
That still the added years may bring
To him their joys : the knell has rung
Alas ! in recent hours,

For one who shared his life's fine task,
Of loving helpfulness to all.

   Come gently, gentle Time,
Dropping soft balsam from thy wing,
Oh, bid the suffering soul aspire

   To heights the more sublime.
Our life is all a mingled woof ;
The laugh leaps up, the tear-drops fall ;

   Lend kindly Heaven thy light,
That we may act our part and sleep ;
Strike out some music from the lyre,

   Then welcome the still night !

But I forget ; accept dear friend
The cordial greeting offered now—

   May truest happiness
Encircle still that ripe old age
That has for its most perfect crown

   Heaven's love, yet owns no less
Man's too, the best of earthly good !
May gentle fingers smooth the brow

   Adorned with silvery hair

In ministry most beautiful
Within the home, and others own
        Without that home, how fair
Th' example of a virtuous life,
And by its pattern shape their deeds.
        Ever with palm in palm
The Past and Future stand, oh may
They sing most clearly to your ear
        Their grandest sweetest psalm !
Accept, dear Sir, this lowly gift,
Devon has nourished from her seeds
        These little snow-white flowers,
Take them and let them be a sign
That to the people you are dear,
        Native to her green bowers !

Torrington,
  29th January, 1883.

SELF-SACRIFICE.

 AWOKE from troubled sleep,
　　In the hush of the solemn night,
　　Through the curtainless window streamed
　The rays of the pale moonlight,
　　All the house was still!

The bird in the nest was mute,
　I heard but the tinkling sound,
In the daisied meadow without
　As it meandered and meandered around,
　　Of a little rill!

In my heart the longing woke,
　For the voice, the touch, the kiss,

Of one that was gone from me.
   All day and all night I long
        For that presence so sweet !

My dearest, my sister, mine own,
   Never, ah ! never more
Comest thou to me to kiss
   From that shadowy far-off shore
        Where linger thy feet !

The twin of my spirit was she,
   We grew like two flowers on a stalk,
And shared still the golden-bright hours,
   In the task, in the study, the walk
        By the glancing sea wave !

She died in her beautiful bloom ;
   She faced a great danger, and said,
"'Tis my duty to do it !" and fell,
   Not regretting her own life was paid
        Another to save !

So I moan in my pain, and cry,
   " Is the light gone out in the dark,

The light of that beautiful life?
　Hath the arrow shot at the mark
　　Fallen in vacant air?"

Was I waking or sleeping just then?
　Warm fingers were clasped about mine,
Gently and firmly and close;
　I saw the glorious eyes shine
　　Through the flowing hair

That fell as a golden veil
　Round the white-robed figure fair!
I knew her, mine own, again,
　As I saw her standing there,
　　And my heart was at rest!

The vanished years came back,　　'
　She was mine as in days of old,
Just herself, the same dear self,
　And seeing, my soul waxed bold:
　　" Dear love, on your breast

Let me lay my weary head."
 Then she spoke in sweet tones and low,
" Shall I sing you a song I love,
 An old sad song whose woe
    Is sweeter than joy ? "

" Dear, sing it," I said, " that song ;
 What you like must I like too.
Oh, sing as you sang that day,
 In the bower where the June roses blew,
    Whose sweets did cloy ! "

This was the lay :
 " Afar in a tower by the sea,
A maiden sitteth.
 Around and around the tower,
The sea-bird flitteth
    All the livelong day !

" Maiden beautiful,
 She dwells in the old grey tower
Under spell of magic,

There dwelleth she till the years
Bring her fate most tragic :
    Meekly dutiful,

" For the gods willed it !
   She looketh toward the east,
Where each new morning
   The sun-rays climbing the skies
With brightest adorning
    Tenderly gild it.

" Around the old tower
   A venomous serpent is twining,
Climbing and clinging
   Closer and higher each year,
While the maiden is singing
    Aloft in her bower.

" Gigantic of size
   He enringeth and twineth the tower,
That mystical dragon,
   Slowly, one coil with each year.
Like wine in a flagon
    Sparkle his eyes !

" When his gold-green crest

   He shall lift to the top of the tower,

Alas, for the maiden,

   No hope, but she falleth his prey !

When the clouds storm-laden

     Sail out of the west,

"They pour down thick rain,

   Such weeping should be for her fate !

Lo ! a white sail is flying,

   A little boat shows afar off,

Now it is hying

     Across the blue main !

" One cometh to save,

   A youth in his beauty and strength ;

He loves the fair lady,

   He comes the fierce dragon to slay

The green palms shady,

     Do proudly wave

" O'er the conqueror's car,

   When he cometh from war with his spoils,

But what shall be given

To him who fighteth alone ?
Lo ! his spear it is driven—
   Ye gods shall he scar

" That gold-plated crest ?
  His spear it is piercing the snake,
He unrolls from the tower
  His great coils, relaxing in death.
The maid in her bower,
   Sings, ' Greatest and best,

" ' Oh bravest of knights ! '
  Alas for the youth, ah, the woe !
Though he slayeth the dragon
  He takes his own hurt to the death.
The years will lag on,
   Slow ripening men's rights,

" But that beautiful youth
  Will champion the helpless no more !
Now he is lying
  Low at the lady's feet,—
Ah ! he is dying,
   Well proven his truth !

" ' From thy prison-tower,
  Daughter of the gods, go free !
Go in thy fair beauty,
  Lift on men thy glorious brow !
Sure it was my duty
    Thus my life to pour.

" ' Weep not thou for me ;
  'Tis a little thing, I die
To save thee, lady.
  Crown thou with a kiss my deed.
To the regions shady
    Bear I thoughts of thee ! '

" So he died that day,
  By the old grey tower by the sea,
But the maiden is living,
  And beauty and joy unto men
She is bounteously giving
    As she goeth her way."

I woke with mine eyelids wet
  With the tears of the happy dream.

In the pale heart of the east,
  Was coming then the first beam
    Of the rosy dawn.

The earth was dewy and fresh,
  With the green sprays waving to and fro ;
In the park, beneath the trees,
  By the silver-footed doe
    Ran the young fawn.

Ah me ! it was but a dream,
  But it lulled the pain at my heart,
So the god-like on earth may be free
  To act out its beautiful part !
    'Tis noble to die !

In the cause of the lofty and true,
  The life that's ungrudgingly given
Is like the rich wine that is poured
  In sacred libation to Heaven
    In sacrifice high.

KENWITH.

PART I.

HERE the long channel broadens its blue
    arm,
Stretched to the main,[1] and rolls its heavy
    waves
Upon the pebbly girdle of the land,
High on its circular mount, with walls enringed,
Uprose the tower of Kenwith, hoar and grey,
Built by some Briton chief in days far back,
Before the Saxon came to power of rule ;
And therein lay Odune, the Devon Earl,
The servant of King Alfred,[2] and with him
A scanty remnant of his following,
Few men, but brave and of determined soul.
They held the place 'gainst the barbaric hordes

Led by the Viking Hubba, Regnor's son,[3]
Of all the Norsemen fiercest and most fell.
With his long ships, from summer raid returned
From the Demetian coast, which he had swept
With fire and sword, harrying the mountain kings,
He anchored on the Devon shore—a tract
As yet unshorn of its rich growths, where spread
Green pastures, and in season waved, full-eared,
The yellow-bearded corn.   Upon the banks
Washed by the mingled Taw and Torridge ere
They pour their tribute waters to the deep,
The troops of the Berseger camped, and reared
On high their standard ; central 'mong their tents,
The giant ensign waved, its voluminous folds
Opening and closing with the wild sea gales.
Sacred was that great gemmed and broidered flag
To the rude war-sons of the north ; their Scalds
Sang of it in wild lays : fabling, they told
How Hubba, son of Lodbrok, in his youth
Received it, wrought by spell in one brief hour,
By the weird three [4] who in the sombre depths
Of a pine-forest suddenly fronted him

With crownèd brows.   From out the hoary gloom,
Exceeding beautiful of face they shone,
Women, but taller than of mortal mould ;
White-raimented, and glistening like the moon,
Silvered with frost.   Chanting the runic lay,
They deftly wove—those pale Queens of the North—
The mighty raven standard, gave it him,
And faded out of sight ; and evermore
He bore it with his armies where he passed,
Throughout all lands ; and ever in the fray
The bird of Odin, wrought thereon by these,
The fateful three, raising the giant wing,
Or drooping it, gave sign of victory
Or loss ; in many a field its blazonry
Had streamed, and round its stand had striv'n and
      fought
Their noblest, bravest !

                    With Odune the Earl,
And with the remnant of his following
Entrenched in the rude fortress, lived that hour
The hope of Alfred's kingdom.   The fair land
Lay in the grasp of the rapacious foe,

Sucked dry of all her wealth : northward, from where
Northumbria stretched her line, to the towered city
Built by the Roman lords of old, and thence,
Beyond the streams of Avon, bordering
The land of the West-Saxons, Alfred's realm,
The barbaric troops had poured, and filled
The ways with blood and violence.   The Saxon King,
Forsaken of his best in that dark strife,
Stood single 'gainst his enemies, and passed,
Crownless and sceptreless, to the marsh wilds
Of Somerset ;[5] and there, in secret hold
Abiding, tarried till his hour should come
To strike once more for throne and kingdom.   Thus
Through all the desolate land one wail went forth :
The glare of temples reddened in the skies,
The peaceful homesteads lay in smouldering heaps,
And still the spoiler spoiled !

                              Near ten decades,
The feet of heathen in the land had bruised
Her fields, and trampled down her fruits, at first
Small pirate bands, roving the restless seas,
Which swooped for plunder on the unguarded coast,

Gorged them and fled ; they slowly gathered head,
And waxing bolder, led their armies on
To sack her cities and pull down her forts.
Oft the strong-handed Saxon lords smote them,
But still the hydra-headed foe afresh
Rose up ; and for her slain and vanquished sons,
The teeming North gave from her breast new sons
To more than fill their place !

                      Men told of signs
Presaging evil, ere the heathen hordes
Poured from their native forests of the North :
In the night heavens a fiery meteor blazed,
Shaped like a crucifix ; [6] each eve it rose,
After the set of sun, stretching its arms
Athwart the western blue ; upon the disc
Of the blanched moon, paling toward the dawn,
Dark spots like drops of sprinkled blood were seen ;
And on the eve of the Nativity,
The year that Egbert set the regal throne
Above the petty princedoms of the land,
Her broad and silver shield, eclipsed, burned red,
With dusky glare, turned wholly into blood.

And there were wondrous adders in the woods
Of Andreds-lea, skirting the Kentish coast,
Where Hengist had his seat of power of old,
Which hissing glid into the homes of men
And wrought them mischief. Thus they spake, and held
Those things prophetic of the direful times
When shrine and altar of the heavenly Christ
Were overthrown and holy place despoiled,
By the red-handed worshippers of Thor.

     *   *   *   *   *   *

Within the chamber of the turret sate
The Saxon chieftain, gazing on the sea,
Seen through the lattice of the tower, broad, smooth,
And darkly blue, with all its level waves
Reposed.   It was the eve ; the sun was low
Upon the waters, and above its disc,
Dark, fiery, hung a single heavy cloud,
Its rough and jagged lines incarnadined
With the red glare beneath.   Beside the Earl
A lady stood, of noble mien, his wife ;
Her face was white and worn, yet beautiful
As some Greek dream of beauty, like the calm

Grand front of Pallas, with the regal brow
Set with the seal of the high soul.   She leant
Upon the chieftain's shoulder, and her eyes,
Like his, were turned toward the great red sun
Slowly descending in the mighty breast
Of waters, crimsoned with the fiery flush
Along the line of waves.   Thus for a while
The twain ; then, turning to his wife, the Earl
Broke silence, saying, " One sole hope remains—
One only ; on it will I stake our all.
Fear not the issue ; we have hewn our way
Through ranks of foes as stout as these which now
Encompass us.

     " Rememberest thou, my wife,
That sunrise on the fatal Wilton hills,
The morning after battle ?⁷   (Thou wast there,
For all night long thou wanderedst o'er the field
Seeking our Saxon dead.)   Not yet the sun
Was risen, but above a pile of clouds
A thin and narrow band of light appeared,
Pale herald of the day.   Then, wearing still
His armour, clotted with the battle-drops,

The King came by, and stood by me and spake :
'What thinkest thou, Odune ; shall in this land
The foe prevail, and all of God be gulfed
In heathen blackness?' and I made reply,
Not wisting what to answer, for mine heart
Was smitten with the sense of our great loss,
'What thinkest thou, my liege ?' He answered not
A moment's space ; then said he, while his eyes
Rested upon that narrow rim of dawn
Which brightened in the heavens, 'I have thought
        much ;
Haply God's purpose broadens slowly through
These bloody times to its full arc of day.
Not Thor, but Christ ; not Dane, nor Saxon, Celt,
Nor Angle, but one people in the land,
And in them all the Christ.' Grieving, I spake,
'Oh, my dread lord, how should this be, for we
Are rather like wild beasts that rend each other ?'
Still gazing on that line of gold, which waxed
And broadened till the hills were bathed in light,
And all the melancholy field revealed,
With its great clumps of slain, the king replied,

' Methinks it will be so.' He added not,
But as he turned I marked his countenance,
Sublime as some great angel's. Still the words
Live in my mind. Can the fulfilment be
Far off or near, of that which Alfred spoke,
Or shall this goodly realm of Christ slide back
Upon the edge of hell, and sink itself
Into the bestial slough, knowing not God?
Bruised underneath the Pagan heel we lie.
Oh, England ! oh, my country ! oh, poor land,
Of thine own sons betrayed !—aliens, not sons.
Shall in the eagle's nest be reared the wren ?
Or at the udders of the lioness
Young hares ? Yet such are we,—even such."

                                        She bent

Closer toward him, and as he spake her cheek
Waxed paler, whiter than the white storm-foam
Borne on the livid wave. Yet her clear eyes
Shone on him in their beauty, as she said,
" Not all, oh Earl ! The winnowing of God
Doth separate the precious from the vile ;

Yet are there left some loyal English hearts,
Enough to raise King Alfred's throne once more
From out its ruins,—such thou hast with thee.
These few most noble ones redeem the base."
" Yea," said the Saxon, " there are that remain,
As precious grains in our great heap of chaff;
Nor deem I that the king's high hopes can fail
Wholly their issues.   The foul Pagan dark
Cannot out-quench the light.   The higher power
Surely subdues the lower.   The human doth
Out-tower the brute, and slowly master it,
Though with long steps of pain.
                                        " But to our task.
My men await my bidding; they will go
Whither I lead; yea, into any gulfs
Of death I choose to leap, they will not blench
To follow.   We will dare all chance, all risk,
And beard this heathen foe; before the dawn,
Under the covert of the early dusk
Make we our sally from the fort."
                                        He paused,
And all his iron will gathered its power

Upon his massive brows, and set the lines
Sterner round the firm mouth ; nor more he said,
Nor she to him replied.   Silent they sate,
Hand clasped in hand, with hearts too passion-fraught
For speech.   The mournful sea moaned in her bed,
Rolling from off the beach her tide, and from
The woods a solitary eagle's cry
Resounded in the stillness ;—such great strain
And stress of agony could come but once
Within a life, even as the death-pang
Doth come but once.   So the slow moments crept.
And then they spoke, in broken passionate words—
Fragments of speech, shivered with the strong pain,
Like riven stones from the hot entrails thrown
Of fiery Ætna, when its sulphurous womb
Heaves with volcanic birth—their farewells.   Rose
They both and stood ; then turned, and hand from hand
Lingeringly drew, and the Earl passed from forth
The turret chamber, and the massy door
Clanged after him.

                    Beneath the edge of cloud
The last red embers of the sunset fires

Faded, and the night fell upon the face
Of the broad waters : the pale stars wheeled forth
Upon their courses to fulfil their paths
In the high heavens ; the moon was not, or young,
And as a colourless crescent gave faint light
To rip the gloom ;—so over all the scene
The descending night her shadowy mantle spread,
Nature's great peace, as ever.

                              Then the Earl,
Moving among his followers, spake, " Arise,
Prepare yourselves, for know my purpose stands
To lead you forth.   Be ready ere the dawn
Plant her pale prints upon the eastern hills.
Haply we may take by surprise the foe,
Who, haughty in his strength, relaxes watch."

*   *   *   *   *   *

Beneath the raven standard, whose large folds
Swayed slowly in the wind, within his tent,
The Berserk sat, carousing with his jarls.
The bearded vikings grim, lolling at ease,
Filled to the brim the horns with fragrant mead,
Trolling the wassail song with clangorous noise,

While rose and rolled the low hoarse laugh, as breaks
The sullen surf upon the jagged rocks
With all their cavernous hollows !
                              Large of frame
And strong of limb were they, these Norseland jarls :
Upon their arms the brawny muscle swelled,
Like gnarled roots of ancient British oaks,
Knotted and large.   Dinted with strokes of war,
Tanned with the winds, those bold sea-rovers ; each
Gaunt form was like a furrow-cloven cliff,
On whose keen ledge the eagle sits at watch,
Or like some granite peak far out at sea,
Wave-washed and rent.
                              So drank the Berserk bold
Huge draughts ; and all the captains of his war
Drank deep with him, and the wild laugh leapt up,
And rang in peals a-down the table ; while
The large and measured horns passed to and fro,
And each man strove his fellow to out drink.
" A goodly land, here will we take our ease
Large woods and pastures, and fair rivers, where
Glance the bright shoals of fish, tumbles and leaps

The large white salmon, foam-like in the foam !
The Sceptre of the Saxons, where is he ?
Ask the wild boars, question the wallowing swine,
If with them herds the sometime Wessex King."
So passed the scornful jest, tossed like a ball
From each to each, nor spared the Devon Earl,
Late foe in arms, whom with his men they deemed
Meshed in their net.   Towered the Norse chief's form,
Uprising ; with his heavy fist he smote
Upon the boards, as some huge hammer strikes
Heavily on the anvil of the smith,
And saying, "We have run the fox to earth,
And he cannot escape us," scoffing laughed,
And laid his massive form again at ease.
And when the lazy laughter of his scorn
Died on his lips, lazily he turned him round,
And his eye lighted on his favourite Scald,
Who stood apart, leaning upon his harp.
An aged man was he, with length of beard
In cataracts of snow tossed o'er his breast,
Down to the girdled waist ; to him the chief
Spake carelessly, raised on his elbow : "Sing ;

Give us one of your sagas; let us hear
The clangour of Thor's hammer as it smites
Upon the rocks, the hurtle and the clash
Of the great gods contending on the plains."
Straightway the hoary Scald bent o'er his harp,
And with his fingers swept the chords, with voice
Accompanying; he sang the ancient strife
Betwixt the Æsir and the giant race,
Waged in the realms of ever-during frost;
And how the hammer of the Thunderer cleft
The mountains to their spurs, rent with their trees
Asunder; and of the great halls of the gods,
And of fair Asgard diademed with towers,
The hundred-gated city which poured forth
Her hosts to battle on the sacred plains,
Her choicest flower of warriors daily slain,
To be with each new morn renewed; then changed,
And like the mournful music of the wind,
'Mong the pine tops, within the vast hoar woods
Of Orkadale, low melancholy flowed
The melodious song, the lay of Balder, first
Of sons of heaven, whom all men did love,

So fair was he, and gentler than the breath
Of spring, first breathing o'er her violets.
Howbeit by craft he fell, and the sun-god
Passed to the shades of Hela.   All the deep
Burned with the great funerëal ship on which
His pallid corse lay decked;[*] far off it shone,
Like the red meteorous blaze which sometimes lights
The sunless heavens of Norroway in deep
Mid-winter—a colossal pyre of fire,
A mount of ruby tipped with gold : while ran
The earth with human tears, more fast than streams
That sudden gush in genial warmth of spring.

But when the strings thrilled to th' impassioned touch,
Suddenly 'neath the hand, the central chord
Snapped, and the music ceased.   Then in the pause
Ensuing, lifting up his glooming brows
'Mong the grand rugged heads that ringed him round,
The Scald said gloomily, " An evil sign ;
I like it not ; oh jarl, sea-king, beware !
The misty remnants of an ominous dream
Trouble my memory ; last night it was,

Methought I stood upon the beach, and gazed
Upon the waters of a turgid sea.
Not this which lips yon belt of pebbly stones,
But the great northern sea, with all her waves
Rolled heavily, as after storm scarce sunk
To rest.   Above the crest of a large wave,
Hollowed and livid green below, uprose
A head, gigantic, armed, the vizor drawn.
Upon the helm, what seemed a kingly crown
Was set; but as I gazed the circlet paled
And vanished utterly, and the crowned head
Descended crownless to the wave; strange runes
Ran wailingly along the deep and died
In silence.   I awoke, and knew my dream
Foreboded evil.   Son of Lodobrok
Beware !"

       He hearkened, the Norse chief; his brows,
Like granite rocks o'erhanging scowling floods,
Grew darker in their wrath ; yet light he laughed,
And, striking with his sword on the harp-strings,
Said, " Dream no more—or dream to better aim.
Let the reft chord be mended ; for the rest,

M

Fear not for us : what the sword wins the sword
Can hold."*
                    And to his men, " Oh, jarls, rest you,
We verge upon the dawn."   He raised the screen
Which parted off the inner tent, passed in,
And on a couch of skins stretched his huge frame ;
The fret-work veinage on his temples sank,
And the broad chest to gentler breathings fell,
And gradually as some large braund dies down
From flame to smouldering brightness on the hearth,
The fiery gleams quenched out and paled themselves
In the deep glowing eyes, and with a low
Bubble of laughter, murmuring brokenly,
Half dreaming, "Hares caught in the gin, safe trapped,"
The hardy northern chieftain sank to sleep,
The slumberous thought of scorn within his heart.

PART II.

It neared the dawn, but yet no shafts of light
Pierced the dull east ; the swathes of a thick mist
Clung closely to the cold face of the earth ;

The leaves were wet as if with heavy rain,
But rain was not, only the sheeted mist
Slowly dissolved itself in clammy drops.
Within the ancient castle's beetling walls,
The men of Kenwith gathered silently
Around their chief; a single torch,
With foggy rings begirt, burned in the midst,
And cast its light upon the warrior's face,
Revealing it like to some early god's,
Divinely calm : and calm, and stern, and set,
The faces which surrounded him, as if
Hewn from the rock, so stamped was every brow
With steadfast purpose ; for they knew, these men,
They moved into the very jaws of death,
Following their leader's call.

      The rivulets
Babbled among their osiers, and the sea
Murmured amid her surges chill and cold.

Then spake Odune, chief of the Saxons, " Rise,
Let us go forth ; follow me close, oh friends !
Strike when I give the word.   Strike, O great heart

For Christ and for the King !"   So outward passed
And underneath the pall of the thick mist
In silent march went on : no clink of sword
Betrayed them, nor the glint of armour shone,
Splintering with rays the dark ; no feather waved
In all the band, nor did they bear aloft
The dragon of the western Saxons, which
Their chiefs and heroes old were wont to bear
In battle.   As the drops of the night-dew
Softly distil upon the delicate flower,
Soundless their motion ; and as silently
And gently as the white curled mist glides up
On a still morn from some smooth river's brink,
Along the grassy marge, they onward moved.
Thus stealthily approached they unperceived
The Norseman's camp.   Between the deadly fans
Of the out-lying lines the Saxons passed,
Close to the ring of dusky tents.   They crept
On hands and knees along the slimy ground,
Each man apart, slowly, with bated breath,
And with enormous toil.   The camp-fires pricked
With spiry flame the dull moist air, and round

About them slept the spearmen of the Dane,
Their arms piled near, while the lax sentinels,
With wassail filled, forbore the wonted watch,
Dreading no foe. So won they way within
The camp of the Dane-King, of him unknown.
The raven standard waved its heavy folds
From the raised staff athwart the shadowy tents,
Dim-gleaming in the dusk ; like the white wing
Of some pale swan gliding the azure wave,
The silver broiderings shone on the huge flag
Woven around the bird of the war-gods.
And now from off the bosom of the sea,
With the incoming tide, a breeze began
To rise, which, blowing softly, freshened still,
And the mist lifted as a curtain lifts,
Suddenly, and the dawn smote on the field,—
The chill faint dawn,—revealing the dark orb
Of tents more clear ; and as the obscured morn
Touched with her melancholy rays the plain,
The careless sentinels, sleeping on watch,
Started, and lifting eye, beheld the foe
Close at their side. Then a great cry went forth,

And voices called to arms; the trumpets brayed,
Hoarse-voiced and deep, and ere the Saxon chief
Could muster round himself his men at arms,
As if the shadowy earth brought forth a crop
Of giant sons, new-sown with dragons' teeth,
The field up-heaved her host of warriors.
Then came he with a shout from forth his tent—
The grim sea-king, the son of Lodobrok!—
A great voice, " Up, jarls, and arm ye l up, Danes,
Kings of the deep!" And shrilled the battle-cry
Of the West Saxons, " Out for holy rood
And for the King!" And Odune formed his men
In order as he best might, being few.
Each Saxon Thane led on his sons and carles.
These, under him, their head, formed into close
And narrowed phalanx, forward moved, to make
Assault upon the foe, who, on his part,
Gathered and fronted with great shields enlocked,
Bristling his lines with points of spears.   Then charge
The Saxons, and with wedge-like force cleft way
Through the thick hostile ranks.   These swerved, an·
          now,

Fierce with great hate, the Dane and Saxon strove,
Man against man, mixed, interwoven, crushed,
In grapple of close fight. So through the morn
The cries of battle rang among the hills
By the grey sea, the while the tardy sun
Arose behind thick bars of heavy clouds,
Between whose openings glared blood-red the light,
As if beneath closed portals slowly oozed
A stream of gore. And fiercely raged the strife,
Nor ceased, nor slacked, until the Saxon band
Was thinned with slaughter, and the northern jarls,
Had man by man, fallen about their flag.
Then, in the midst of a great ring of slain,
'Mid tumbled helms and shields to pieces hacked,
The Saxon saw his foeman standing. Proud
He towered his height, unhelmed his head, and loose
His tawny lion-like locks flowed to the wind.
Down at his feet was dropped the large round shield,
Silvered, as the pale moon upon a lake
Uprisen, but his grasp retained the axe,
The dread war-weapon of the northern kings.
Toward him advanced Odune the Earl, nor paused,

Though spent with toils of fight, and dyed with bloo
Of foemen, redder than the flame-hued sun,
Which from the shoulders of the enormous clouds
Ascended eastward, while the battle passed
With thunderous shoutings 'long the hilly banks
Skirting the coast.   Over the heaps of dead
The Saxon warrior stepped, and planted foot
Facing his foe ; nor turned that chieftain grim,
But moveless as a rock awaited him
With front of pride.   But when the Ealdor saw
More near the pallor of the unhelmed brow,
And how the mighty frame, steadfast at first,
Began to sway, as some Norwegian pine
Rocks slowly to and fro, when in a gale
The furious wind tugs at the deep-fanged roots—
(For he was wounded with a grievous hurt—)
The noble heart was touched within his breast
With pity, and, saying, " Oh, mine enemy,
Accept thy life ;" he bent toward him, and sheathed
Straightway with generous hand the sword he bore.
But the Dane answered not, nor vouched reply,
But knotted into frowns his haughty brows

Heavy with anger. Suddenly he bowed
Toward the earth, then with swift motion drew
Erect his stature ; on his forehead swelled
The purple veinage, and the muscles rose·
Quivering and large on the magnific frame,
Strained to the utmost. Quick he raised the axe,
With fierce two-handed clutch, the knuckles large
And whitened with their grip, hurling his blow
Straight at the Saxon's undefended breast.
But ere the flashing axe, whirling aloft,
Cut through the air descending, Odune saw
The imminent peril, and though waxen faint
With wounds which bled unheeded in the strife,
Stepped quickly back ; but moving, smote his heel
Upon a broken sword-blade on the ground,
And swerved thereby, dropped to his knee on earth,
And over him up-towered the grisly jarl.
In act to strike he stood, when one who served
The Devon Prince came in between the twain,
Shielding his fallen lord from his fierce foe
With the exposure of his own unmailèd breast—
A carle of the Earl's house ; youthful he seemed,

And slender-moulded as a woman's was
The supple form in its light coat of hide.
On him, the devoted liegeman, fell the stroke
Aimed at his lord ; through nerve and bone it shore
Even to the seat of life.   But he who smote
Staggered a step or two backward, and sank
At foot of the great standard of the host.
There lay beneath the shadow of the folds,
And threw his angry eyes upon the Earl
Scowling vehement hate, balked of his prey.
Half from the ground he reared his massive bulk,
Lifted his right arm, and a hoarse sound rolled
Like laughter from his lips,[10] deep volumed, hoarse,
As crashing of the billow when it curls
Its livid greenness in the wild north sea
Into more livid white of angry foam,
So from his lips that laugh.   It ceased, and passed
Into the silences of death ; he dropped
Heavily forward on the blood-stained ground.

So fell the heathen King before his flag,
And his men panic-stricken fled the field ;

As a great mass of snow, hung on the breast
Of some vast Alp, upon a sudden slips
With thunderous sound down to the mountain's base,
The pagans broke and fled ; with cries like howls
Of the strong storm in a dense forest where
No foot of man doth come, shrieking 'twixt rows
Of twisted trees : precipitate they fled,
And gat them to their ships moored on the strand,
Nor tarried.

    Over the crushed piteous corse,
A piece of bleeding wreck, of that young slave
Who died to save his lord, bent the great Earl
Grievingly, and with gentle hands unlaced
The tight drawn casque, disclosing the white face
Whose lineaments of delicatest mould
Showed in their native nobleness most pure.
A lovely face was it, crowned with soft rings
Of paly golden curls about the brow—
Lovely yet awful, the smile on the lips
Frozen by death ; and the Earl stood at gaze,
Anchoring his steadfast eyes upon its cold
Serenity. He did not stir nor move,

But his face slowly changed, as told in myths
Wondrous of old-world bards, theirs changed who
          looked
Upon the beautiful horror of the face
Gorgonic ; cold, stone-like, rigid as death,
Pale as the terrible white polar seas,
When o'er their ribs of icebergs, the lean bears,
Shiveringly, in the Arctic's winter's cold,
Pass to and fro.   Anon he drew aside
The riven pieces of the leather hide
Covering the mangled flesh, and moving them,
Revealed to sight the breasts of woman, crushed,
Battered, yet visibly the large twin orbs
Which once were lovelier than hills of snow,
Or lilies touched with morning's first pale pink.
Upon those mangled breasts the warrior bowed
The grandeur of his head, with a great cry,
Sharp as of one who feels the sword pass through
His loins death-wounded ; so he cried and bowed
Lowly the helmèd grandeur of his head.
Anon he raised himself and to his thanes,
Who gathered round in silent reverence,

Noting the greatness of his sorrow, turned,
And saying simply : " It is my wife ; she
Hath followed me into the battle, and given
Her own life for my sake," bowed him again
Over his dead, and his hands wanderingly
Passed o'er the beauty of the face, as one
Blind feels the statue, seeking by the touch
To inform the mind, closed at the gates of sight
From knowledge.   O'er the brow and lips and hair
Strayed softly those strong battle-hardened hands,
Dyed with red stains.   So long he dumbly knelt
By the crushed body, that the faithful thanes,
Fearing to touch the precincts of a woe
So dread, looked each on each in silent doubt,
Till one approached the Earl, a soldier who
Had loved the Earl his father in old days,
A hard and wrinkled man, but sweet of heart,
And laying on his hand his own, while tears
Dropped from his aged eyes, said : " Dear my lord,
Remember England and the King ; to them
As a flower-wreathèd sacrifice to Heaven
Is offered up this sacred woman-life ;

Think of it so, and be consoled."   The Earl
Lifted himself thereat, and 'neath his feet
The solid earth seemed heaving, as a boat
Rocks underneath the feet of one unused
To the rough dancing of the wild sea's breast ;
Yet calmly spake, and curbed th' internal pangs,
As a strong hand controls a wild war-steed
Furious with pain.   "Yea," said the Earl, " enough ;
Cover from sight the face of my dead wife,
I cannot longer look thereon and be
As man should be.   Call back pursuit, and show
Mercy to these the vanquished.   To the fort ;—
Take up the body, lay it tenderly
Upon your shields, so ; let us hence, oh friends,
Sharers of mine heart's sorrow ! "

                                        The grey sea
Rocked in her bed, and lifted up her voice,
Mystic and wonderful.

                              So in slow march
Toward the fortress-rock passed on the thanes,
Bearing the noble dead ; and 'long the ranks,
From man to man through all the Saxon band,

There went a sound of mourning, like the cry
Of melancholy birds, heard in the night
Flitting across the dim and misty wolds.
And all the women of the castle wept,
Issuing from out the gates [11] to meet the bier
Of their dead lady, and they kissed her face,
Lifting the veil from off the solemn brows :
Kissed it, and wept, bitterly, loud and long.

* * * * * *

The night had darkened o'er the battle-field
And o'er the antique tower, and silence was.
Upon the borders of the lonely shore,
The fallen chieftain's grave was made,
And over it was heaped a cairn of stones,
According to the wont of burial
Of the old kings of Northland : in the dim
And clouded night, empty of noises, save
The plashing of the waves upon the beach,
Stood by the grave the Norse chief's ancient scald.
His lean gaunt form was leaner and more gaunt,
All shrivelled as a lightning-blasted pine
Whose bark is bleached and dry ; moveless he stood

Within the shadow of the tumulus,
Silently thus a while, and then began,
Moving with measured pace round the grey cairn
To chant a weird, wild rune, mournfully low,
A song, as 'twere, all fraught with human tears.
And when the chant had dragged its length and died,
The ancient saga-man turned from the grave
And bent his heavy steps toward the beach,
Where floated on the waters, large and dark,
The esk of Hubba, with the dragon crest
Carved on the prow, gold scaled, and by its side
The smaller war-craft, empty, silent all,
With idly flapping sails (for they that fled
The sword which hacked them flying, the red field,
Seizing the foremost of their ships, had put
To sea, delaying not).   The wrinkled scald
Looked on the large-ribbed barque, and on the line
Of drooping sails shadowing the midnight wave,
With eyes of mournful ire, and murmuring :
" It is the twilight of the gods, the dread
Regnorock, let the great earth rive her sides,
And topple down her cities to the grim shades,

Of mist-swathed Hela," clenched his lean hard palms
Driving the claw-like nails deep in the flesh.

Beside the esk a little boat lay moored,
Held by a chain thereto : a slender skiff,
Without or sail or rudder, without oars.
Muttering his words of doom, the saga-man
Approached the boat, and, loosening the chain
Which held it to the esk, he stepped therein.
He stood, he turned, with long lean arms outstretched,
Bending his face toward the burial place
Of the dead King and his fall'n warriors :
" Last of a line of chiefs, from Odin sprung,
Great chief and brave, the Valkyrs call thee up
To feast in wide Valhalla, and to quaff,
From cups of skulls, thine enemies' warm blood,
If that the trumpets of Regnorock yet
Delay to sound the direful day of doom !"
So spake, and pushed the boat from off the shore,
And seaward passed, into the hungry dark,
And no man saw him any more.

                              There stood,

N

Not far removed from the old Castle's seat,
Westering, a hillock; on its crown a grove
Of trees, which, hearse-like, waved against the line
Of golden cloud, when the great star of day
Rolled on the waters his bright wheels of flame,
Nightly descending.   There the wind sang soft
Among the muffling trees, with faint low stops,
A sorrowful hymn, when, as the third morn rose,
Weeping with showers upon the saddened earth,
They laid the lady of Devonia low
Beneath the shadow of the tender boughs,
Wetting the wet earth of her grave with tears.
Pearl of all women, noblest, best of wives,
They named her; not more true Alceste, who,
For love of him she spoused, being great of soul,
Descended to the nether shades, where dwell
The dead of old; nor her made sacrifice
By the rash Gileaditish Prince's vow,
The virgin of Israel, whom Hebrew maids
Yearly with songs lamented.   Shine star-like
From the pale night of death, oh noblest name
Of women! The great glory born of thee

Shall light the rim and dusk of aftertime
With radiance, and our sons to be shall call
Thee bless'd.   Thus they, the Wessex Thanes,
Their shining armour dimmed with rain of tears;
While women's voices shrilled along the dawn
With funeral music.

                                        Sorely hurt
With gashes taken in the grisly fight,
Odune the Earl lay stricken nigh to death,
Muttering and wailing ever in his pain,
Unweeting of the things his dry lips spake;
For a great fire burned at the core of life,
And fumed the wholesome brain with mists of dreams
Fantastic.   Babbled he of fields and woods,
And pleasant streams that ran by shadowy trees,
The waters lily-snowed; anon, across
The whirling phantasy of his dimmed mind
Terror and darkness drifted; the long shriek,
And pass'd the heathen, with a thousand spears
Flashed;—then the dream remade itself to beauty.
So they who listened gathered from his words,
Which told of his own halls, and her who came,

The girl-bride to his home.   So tossed and throbbed
The fevered soul.   But when the seventh night
Paled its bright moon, wax'd to the perfect shield,
Passing into the grey of earliest dawn,
He raised himself from off the wolf-skin couch,
And leaning heavily on his servant's arm,
Drew to the lattice of the turret-tower,
And gazed therefrom across the dim blue sea,
Knowing the desolation of his life,
Stripped bare and lone ; weakened, but clear of mind.

He looked upon the wide breast of the sea,
Touched with the first gold of the climbing lights,
And on the bridal earth, veiled in her dews,
While now the fleecy east flushed its red rose
Of dawning (for the rains were overpast,
And in the fields the flowers began to blow,
Faint sweet, and voice of birds was in the groves),
And knew that there had passed from out his life
Its glory, and from the earth and from the seas
Their glory ; yet knew in his deepest soul
That the great purpose of his life changed not,

And wasted not—no, not a single jot.
And as the strong man after sickness runs
His fingers o'er his arm to find if that
The muscle swell its loops and knots as wont,
Before he close in grapple with his foe,
He felt his higher purpose, and uprose,
God's warrior-servant, ready as erst to strive
In service of the King, against the might
Of heathen breaking flood-like on the land,—
The hordes of Thor.
     Then, ere his hurt was whole,
There went a Bode from the great Earl, and bore
To Alfred, then in hiding in the thick
Of the entangled woods of Somerset,
The tidings of the victory, saying: "Oh King,
Thine enemies are smitten, and their flag
Ravenna taken; it is in our hands—
The standard of the north, the sign of Thor. '
The power of the war-god unto its base
Is shak'n, for the meek Christ doth live and reign
And is the greater!"
     And when the feathery trees

Began to spread the full green fan of leaf
In the far-stretching woods, about the time
Men celebrate the rising from the dead
Of the immortal life,[12] the King went forth,
Leading his followers from their secret hold.
To Egbert's stone he rode; and thither came
To the great forest-heart, the men of Wilts
And Somerset, their thanes and earldormen,
All such as had not fled beyond the seas
For terror of the Pagans; and the King
Cheered them, and heartened them, and, moving
        through
The dim woods, at the dimly-glimmering dawn
Pitched camp in open space, and there unfurled
His standards, near the wooded heights where lay
The army of the North, under their chief,
Guthrun the aged. Him the Christian King,
Heading his troops, gave straightway battle to,
And drove him back with rout unto his forts.
Then sued for peace the heathen, and their chief,
With thirty of his best, swore to the King
Submission; who received their oaths, and gave

To them large grace, and king-like, saying : " Go,
Settle yourselves within our eastern shires ;
There dwell in peace, and sow the fields with seed,
And reap their increase ; learn the dignity
Of labour ; live ye there in peace, O Danes,
Serving the Christ under one yoke with us."

So the great Saxon made secure his seat,
Bastioned on truth and righteousness, and built
The greatness of a kingdom up, to rise
Rock-like amid the roll of centuries,
A grandeur of the earth.   To him his own
Grew like a fruitful vine ; beneath his sway,
His poor had rest, for those clear eyes discerned
Beneath the peasant's lowly vest, the divine one,
The son of God, though named slave of the soil.
The ever-jarring princelings of the land,
Who tangled into knots the web of power,
He set at one, and 'neath his guiding hand
Made of their loose divergent sways one whole
Of kingliness, pacific rule and strong,
Perfect as bridal music.   His strong arm

Smote the fierce heads of riot, as they rose,
Raised by the lawless heathen from the north
Surging, or lifting up themselves again
Within the realm, and under foot pressed them,
And bruised their power.   The sweet arts, flower-like,
Opened, and ampler lights of learning spread
Themselves within the cloisters of the land,
Heretofore darkly wrapped in ignorance.
The East stretched out her hands unto the Prince
Of Saxons, and his pioneers went forth,
Piercing the icy bars of unsunned seas,[19]
Where stream the meteors o'er the shifting bergs,
Varying their splendours.   Large his aims and high,
And alway pure ; so lived and wrought his work,
And passed, but left behind that work to stand
Thro' all the centuries, a kingdom's base
Of power, until the kingdoms of this world
Pass into the one kingdom of the Christ.

NOTES TO KENWITH.

Note 1, p. 133.
"Where the long channel broadens its blue arm,
Stretched to the main."

HE spot which tradition assigns as the site of
the old castle of Cynuit (Kenwith), is in the
neighbourhood of Westward Ho, on the coast
of North Devon, where a long pebbly ridge,
extending by the sea-shore, forms one of the
most remarkable features of the West of England.

There are no vestiges whatever remaining of the old
castle on the circular hill on which it is supposed to have
once stood ; but this is not surprising, considering the
lapse of a thousand years, and the few remains of Saxon
buildings of whatever description we possess ; for, unlike
the Romans and the Normans, the Celts and Saxons
built their forts and castles in the rudest possible manner,
and the masonry of the walls of the old fortress of Cynuit,
of which Asser writes, wherever situated, would not have
been of a character to stand the wear and tear of centuries.

In all likelihood the traditionary site is the correct one,
the historical evidence going far to confirm it. It is such
a place as some Celtic chieftain or Saxon ealdorman

might have chosen in the old times whereon to erect his stronghold, from whose turret-tower his glance could sweep the wide breast of the blue waters opening to the broad Atlantic.

Traditions lingering in the locality point to the scene of the battle between the Saxons and the invaders, and to the burial place or tumulus of the Danish chieftain, Hubba, the leader of the Northmen, on the borders of the bay, where the little town of Appledore now stands.

In former years several large stones lay scattered about near the spot, one of immense size, named the Hubba stone, but they have long since disappeared, and only the finger of tradition points to the place where the chief of the wild Norsemen was laid, together with his warriors, by the quiet and wave-washed shore.

NOTE 2, p. 133.

"—— Odune, the Devon Earl,
The servant of King Alfred."

The historical accounts of the Devon Earl are very brief, but sufficient to show him to have been a man of high and fearless soul, a true hero, whom Devonia may well be proud to reckon among the number of those noble sons of whom she has good cause to glory. *Ethelwerd's Chron.* contains a brief mention :

"In the same year (878) arrived the brother of the tyrant Hingwar, with thirty galleys, in the western parts of the Angles, and besieged Odda (Odune), Duke of Devon, in a certain castle."

Asser gives fuller particulars relating to the besiegement of the castle, without, however, mentioning the name of the leader of the Saxons, Odune, the Ealdor of Devon. See Asser's *Life of Alfred*, under date of the year 878.

NOTE 3, p. 134.

"Led by the Viking Hubba, Regnor's son."

Hubba was one of the three sanguinary sons of Regnor, a prince of the Danes, surnamed Lodobrok, a personage who figures largely in Scandinavian history and fable, to whom some extraordinary feats are attributed, among others that of slaying a monstrous dragon which encircled with its folds the rock-hewn tower of Thora, a princess descended of the race of Æsir; the hero delivered the captive damsel and took her for his wife. Regnor is said to have met his death in a cruel manner at the hands of Ella, a Saxon chief of Northumbria, and his vindictive sons are supposed to have been actuated with the desire of avenging his death in the cruelties they practised on the Saxon people.

NOTE 4, p. 134.

"The weird three."

I.e. The Norns, or the Northern Fates. They are described as three beautiful maidens who sit by the tree of life and guard it, *yggdrasil*, the great world-tree, whose roots and branches are being continually gnawed, but as continually renewed. They allot the destinies of men.

We find them under another aspect, as the Valkyrs, the three war nymphs of Odin, the choosers of the slain, who are present on the battle-field, and conduct the heroes to the feast in the halls of the gods.

The three weird sisters of Shakspere will no doubt occur to the reader, as well as the three queens of a living poet, each different presentations of the rulers of the secret forces of destiny.

NOTE 5, p. 136.
" —— And passed,
Crownless and sceptreless, to the marsh wilds
Of Somerset——"

At the time when Alfred was forced to seek a hiding-place in the marshy isle of Athelney, in Somerset, the Saxons were reduced to the lowest extremity of misery, the whole country being overrun and pillaged by various bands of the Danes, the dispirited people offering no resistance to the cruel despoilers of their homes. The following from the *Saxon Chron.* will give some faint idea of the state of the unfortunate country.

"878. This year, during mid-winter, after twelfth-night, the army stole away to Chippenham, and overran the land of the West-Saxons, and sat down there, and many of the people they drove beyond the sea, and of the remainder, the greater part they subdued and forced to obey them, except King Alfred ; and he, with a small band, with difficulty retreated to the woods and fastnesses of the moors."

NOTE 6, p. 137.
" —— A fiery meteor blazed,
Shaped like a crucifix."

" The sign of Our Lord's Cross appeared in the heavens after sunset," (773) *Ethelwerd's Chron.* See also *Saxon Chronicle*, etc., for this and the other phenomena, which, according to the superstitious belief of the Saxon people, were prophetic of the evil calamities of the heathen invasion.

NOTE 7, p. 139.
" That sunrise on the fatal Wilton hills
The morning after battle."

The Saxon arms met a disastrous defeat on the field of

Wilton about six years previous to the engagement re-
corded in the poem.

NOTE 8, p. 148.

> "——— All the deep
> Burned with the great funerëal ship on which
> His pallid corse lay decked."

Odin caused the body of Balder the beautiful and
beloved to be adorned and laid in state on the deck of a
large ship, which was then set fire to.   The vessel floated
away in flames over the great waters to the regions of
perpetual mists.   The passing of the sun-browed god to
the shades of death is no doubt the symbolization of the
going down of the setting sun, sinking amid his fires upon
his ocean-bed to the darkness of night.

NOTE 9, p. 150.

> "What the sword wins, the sword
> Can hold."

There is reason to suppose that Hubba contemplated a
settlement in Wessex.   His brother Halfdene had already
portioned out the lands of Northumbria among his fol-
lowers, and the Danes had effected a settlement in the
eastern parts of England, as well as in the midland
districts.

NOTE 10, p. 158.

> " Lifted his right arm, and a hoarse sound rolled
> Like laughter from his lips."

It was a frequent boast of the wild warriors of the North
that they would die laughing.   Indeed, to them death on
the battle-field presented no terrors, but, on the contrary,
was a thing to be greatly desired, as it secured an imme-
diate entrance to the halls of Odin, while those who died
ingloriously, by reason of sickness or old age, passed to
the dolorous vales of Hela.

NOTE 11, p. 163.

"And all the women of the castle wept,
    Issuing from out the gates."

Florence of Worcester states that "Many of the king's
thanes, *with their families*, had shut themselves up in the
fortress for protection."

NOTE 12, p. 169.

"And when the feathery trees
Began to spread the full green fan of leaf
In the far-stretching woods, about the time
Men celebrate the rising from the dead
Of the immortal life."

I.e. The Easter of 878, a few weeks after the victory
of Kenwith, which probably occurred in the month of
March.

"Meanwhile, after Easter of that year (878), King Alfred
fought against the army that was in Chippenham, at a
place called Ethandune, and obtained the victory, and
after the decision of the battle the barbarians promise
peace, ask a truce, give hostages, and bind themselves by
oath ; their king submits to be baptised, and Alfred the
King receives him from the laver in the marshy Isle of
Athelney."—*Ethelwerd's Chron.* See also Asser, *Life of
Alfred, Florence of Worcester*, and *Saxon Chron.* for
fuller particulars of the decisive victory of Alfred over the
pagans at this time.

NOTE 13, p. 172.

"The East stretched out her hands unto the Prince
    Of Saxons, and his pioneers went forth,
    Piercing the icy bars of unsunned seas."

Alfred sent help to missions in India, and is said to
have sent out explorers to the arctic seas.

BALDER.

ALDER the beautiful in Asgard fell;
    Him did all living things swear not to
        harm,
All trees, all birds, all beasts, were under spell,
    All earth and air owned the great charm !

The mistletoe alone no worship paid
    Of all that breathes, or moves, or greens the earth,
And by its slender shaft was lowly laid
    Of the great heavens the noblest birth !

He fell, and there was weeping in the plain
    Of Ida, and they wept for many days ;
He fell, and Hela claimed her prey : not slain
    In war, he passed to her dim ways

And made abode among the dead.   Then spake
   The goddess-mother, she who drew all life
From out her breast, " He will no more awake,
   No more be glorious in the strife

Where gods with giants contend.   Ho ! which of you
   Among the doleful shades will seek my son ?
Which of you dare dread Hela's gates pass through,
   So that the god from death, be won ? "

She spoke ; then rose Hermode the swift of foot,
   " I will go seek the mighty dead," he said,
" I, even I, will go ; " and all the gods stood mute,
   Stricken with grief for him low laid.

He took the horse of Odin, the great steed,
   More fleet than rushing winds; nine days, nine nights,
He travelled through th' abyss, nor slacked his speed,
   Till through the darkness dawned dim lights

Faint, pale, a misty twilight which revealed
   Above a gloomy flood, a single arc
Of mightiest span ; the waters lay congealed
   And cold ; there never the swift barque

Might pass, or vessel plough the murky wave,
    The ever-silent river of the dead !
O'er the dread bridge he urged his steed, nor gave
    One pause till its gigantic head

Upreared, with northern front, the awful gate
    Of Hela's halls, wide yawned its doors, he passed
Within, then spake the spectral queen, " But late
    In many a mighty squadron massed

" The countless dead passed o'er yon bridge, yet shook
    Nor echoed not its arch, but thou did'st make
The crashing thunders roll the deep, thy look
    Is that of those who joyful wake

" The glories of the strife.   Whence comest thou ?
    And what thy mission here ?"   He made reply,
" Balder seek I, he of the sun-bright brow,
    Who wrapped in thy cold mists doth lie !

" Yield back thy prey ; him all the weeping gods
    Do crave of thee, thou sovereign of the dead !
Behold the nations tremble 'neath their rods,
    These sue to thee, O queen most dread !"

o

She answered him, "Weep they ? go thou and say,
   Let gods and men, let every creature weep,
Let the whole world run tears, and in that day
   Shall he go free whom else I keep.

" But if one thing refuse to weep, I hold,
   Yea, hold him to the end of days."   Then passed
Hermode to the great Odin, and he told
   The words of the pale queen.   The vast

And hundred-gated city made one wail
   Of weeping, and the earth wept, and each flower,
Each nestling bird, each beast, all in the dale,
   All on the hills mourned in that hour !

As when the frozen earth, touched by the warm
   Sweet breath of spring makes all her rivers flow,
So ran that rain of tears, yet one wrought harm,
   By malice moved to work them woe

Who dwelt in Ida, weeping not when all
   Gave tears ; so the pale Hela kept her prey,
In vain the sacred cities wailed his fall,
   The ages roll,—she holds her sway !

Yet shall he come again and build his throne
 In Asgard, when the days are ripe, there make
His forehead like the sun girt with its zone
 Of rays, and all his prowess take.

NIGHT AND DAY.

"WHAT of the night and day?" he asked
    Who questioned of the sage of old
    The secrets of the universe,
  And cause of things, and thus was told:

" Chief of the great primordial powers
  Rose one, a woman giant-born,
They gave her name, Night, dark-browed Night,
  Night of the sable locks unshorn!

" Not then was sea, nor land; no star
  Shot forth its ray in heaven; the moon
Hung not its silver lamp on high,
  Nor made the sun its fervid noon.

" 'Mong the frost-giants had she home.
  With one of them she wed ; by him
Conceived, and when her time was come
  Brought forth a daughter, Earth.   The dim

" Times spun their course, he died, her spouse,
  Then she espoused one of the race
Of Æsir, and with him 'mong gods
  Made dwelling.   Beautiful of face

" Was he ; and unto him she bore,
  Like to himself, a son most fair.
More goodly child was never born
  In heavenly household ; his bright hair

" Did with a glory crown his brows ;
  He stood before the gods and they
Did own him fair.   They gave him name
  According to his nature, Day,

" Sweet Day, the golden bright-browed Day !
  Well pleased the great Al-fader smiled,
And in him took delight ; he smiled
  Approval of the beauteous child ;

" And unto him he gave in sign
    Of favour a white-wingèd steed,
And bade him ride in orbits round
    The spacious sky with unslaked speed ;

" And to the mother likewise gave
    The kingliest of the gods a steed,
Coal-black, of mighty moulded limbs,
    Such as might serve untired her need,

" And bear her round the measured space
    In the appointed course.   So they,
The mother and the wondrous child,
    Do ever track the selfsame way.

" She first doth ride,—for she was first ;—
    And when, her mighty journey done,
She feeds her steed in Ida's vale,
    On the ambrosial food, her son

" Speeds forth ; the gleaming gates of Morn
    Open to give him way, he moves
Majestic through the firmament,
    And all his lofty prowess proves,

" In eyes of the beholding gods.

  So run the twain their mighty course,

For thus hath Odin willed, and they

    Obey.   From the great phantom-horse

" The woman rides, each morning fall

  The beaded drops that dew the ground ;

They from the panting courser's bit

    Roll down when he doth touch the bound

" And limit of his course.   The white

  And beauteous steed that Day bestrides

Shakes from his mane o'er heaven and earth

    Sweet rays of light, great glory-tides

" Of splendour, brightening all the fields

  Of space.   So do they keep their way,

Nor swerve aside, nor faint nor flag,

    The regent-powers of night and day !"

NIORD AND SKADDA.

TWO voices spake,
    One of the seas, one of the hills,—
    Thus said great Niord the river-god :
    " My rest I make
Beside the waters that I love,
Where sing to me the wild white swans.
    There do I take
Delight ; how beautiful the seas,
The river's arrowy rush, the spread
    Of the smooth lake,
On which the heavens come down with moon
And stars ! in mine own realm I dwell.
    Can I forsake
For thee, Oh daughter of the hills,
The wide, free-flowing deep, whose shores

I haunt, to make
Abode with the night-prowling wolves,
With thee among thine own dim hills ? "

Then a voice spake ;
Thus said the daughter of the hills
In answer : " How can I repose
With thee, and make
My rest upon the sea-god's couch,
When flocks of forest-birds, each morn
Returning, take
Captive my ear with sounds of home?
How can I find delight to dwell
Beside the lake,
Or by the murmuring stream thou lov'st ?
No more ; get thee a river-spouse.
Not for thy sake
Will I forego mine ancient joys.
I bind my skates, I take my bow
Once more, and make
Chase of the beasts that haunt the wilds,
Among mine own loud-echoing hills.

THE VALKYRS.

HE three with helmèd brows shot through
    the night;
Spectral their steeds, more pale than the
    wan light
Which lives above the clouded moon. With shield
Uplift they rode, and o'er the direful field,

Where lay the hero-king, fall'n with his dead,
Passed swift. Then spake the chiefest, the most dread
Of the war-nymphs of Odin, first in power
Of these the fateful three which rule the battle hour;

Leaning upon her lance, she spake : " Behold,
The circle of the exulting gods shall fold
One hero more ; the prince of men shall bring
His warrior-train to Asgard's halls, and king

" Among the great world-kings shall sit him down."
This heard, where with the glittering jewelled crown
About his brows low lay the smitten chief.
He heard, and to the nymphs thus said in grief:

" Lo ! these mine hosts, with them we overthrew,
Have fall'n ; one doom hath wrapped us both ; we slew,
And slaying, fell. Ye whose pale tresses take
The moony beams as in the wind they shake,

" Ye fates ! were we not worthy to achieve
More perfect victory ? " Then they : " We weave
The destinies, and we did smite thy foes
With utter loss ; we gave strength to the blows

"With which thine arm did quell their pride." Then thus
Gondola to her nymphs : " He gave to us
High charge in synod of the thronèd powers.
Pass we to where vast Asgard rears her towers,

" And say, ' Behold, great Odin, the approaching king ;
Him, as thou bad'st us, to thine halls we bring.'
Come, let us urge our steeds on to yon worlds
Where roam the mighty gods." They shook their curls

Loose on the wind, and darted through the night.
Then from his halls did Odin send the light,
Swift-footed Hermode, saying : " Go, attend
Upon his way yon warrior-chief, my friend.

" Greet him with honours like a god, and say
The champions in Valhalla wait, and stay
The listed fight that they may welcome thee."
So sent he him, for fleet of foot was he,

And he did pass, swifter than falling star.
Then Hacon came, red with the stains of war ;
The starry bosses of his shield were dimmed,
And all his golden armour dashed and grimed

With clots of gore.   To him the heavenly powers
Gave welcome large, and where uplifts her towers
The sacred citadel, great Ida's crown,
In circle of the gods he sat him down.

THE' GOD OF THE WINDS.

IKE to some eagle in a lonely land
Which clasps the rugged peak of the huge
crag,
Northward upon the edge of the great heavens
He sits ; he lifts his giant wings, he spreads
His pinions : from them rush earthward the winds.

LIFE.

 WALKED in woods at Easter-tide,
And noted how the tender shafts of
green
Pushed from the boughs, while far and wide
Mixed with the delicate moss the wild flowers' sheen
Spangled the ground !

Waked by sweet touch from sleep, the earth
Felt her delicious life, and crowned with flowers—
Of her deep heart the glorious birth—
With throb of joyous wings in all her bowers,
Sprung to the sound

Of her Creator's voice of love !
Zoned with her young fresh buds, beauteous and fair.
The mighty mother round her wove
Still more of life, more rich, more full, more rare,
The wealth of God !

A while ago, lapped in her snow,
　Like a pale corse she lay, on whose cold lips
The breath plays not, but now the glow
　Of daisies with their tender blushing tips
　　　　　Brightened the road !

A while ago, stricken and mute,
　But now her thousand voices carolled forth
Jubilant songs, and like a lute,
　Sweet-toned and tender and of priceless worth,
　　　　　Warbling flowed her streams !

Life evermore renewed from death,
　Life in its beauty won from the grim tomb,
With sweetness of the new warm breath,
　Brought forth from out the dark and breathless womb
　　　　　Of its chaotic dreams.

So real, warm and sweet to touch,
　So beautiful as with the kiss of God !
We shape it still, and dare avouch
　The spiritual thought in us, which looms so broad
　　　　　Substance and power,

The kernel of all outward things ;
  This vision of the death-won deathless life.
We name it in the Christ, it flings
  From Him its radiance o'er the awful strife
              Of our life's hour !

Nor less the thinkers of old time
  Bodied it forth in legends wild and grand :
The Persian in his creed sublime,
  The Grecian in the fables of his land,
              Gave it a being.

Changing and multiform the waves,
  But one the sea, through all the human tribes
Differing, yet the one truth it saves,
  And in it all fair hope imbibes,
              For dimly seeing

The faint day-dawn on the high hills,
  Watchers in many places as we stand,
We eastward turn, or like the rills,
  'Seaward that flow through all the spacious land,
              We bend one way.

Hither in Thee the streams are met,
  So think we, Christ, oh living deathless One !
Toward Thee the human still is set,
  Watching and yearning till its goal be won,
         Its summer-day.

JAIRUS' DAUGHTER.

LAY her hands upon her breast :
    Oh the rapture of her rest !
    Smile the lips as they were wont ?—
only with a tenderer smile.
Hush ! be still ; surely she but sleeps a little while !

The closed lids of those sweet eyes
Presently will ope and rise,
And their inner lights reveal ;—seem they not to
    quiver now,
As they were about to lift, and those hidden glories
    show ?

But her brow is marble cold,
And her tresses of pale gold

Lie upon her breast, stirless with its heave or fall.
      The soft light
Of the silver hanging lamps streams upon that face so
      white.

      Woe, alas ! for she is dead !
      Throw the lilies on her bed,
Bid the mourners raise their dirge ! weep, oh mother !
      for your child,
Weep the lately springing hopes so strong and wild

      Of the coming Kingly One
      Who the spoils from death hath won,
Healing with a touch the sick, speaking words of
      mightiest power.
Oh ! the hopes, the fears, the passionate longings of
      that hour

      When she hung above her child,
      Though her face was calm and mild
For her gentle darling's sake ! Weep, oh ! stricken
      mother, weep ;

Shear one tress of hair,—this is all of what was thine
      to keep.

    Hush ! weep not, He cometh now !
    Mark the sadness on His brow ;
And His voice—how full of ruth those low tones of
      wondrous power,
Sweet to the heart as summer's breath upon the flower !

    Can the mournful mother guess
    That a love than hers no less,
Greater perhaps, and more divine, lives in Him, the
      stranger there
That in all that mighty grief He no lesser part doth
      bear ?

    By the bed He takes His stand,
    The caressing of His hand
Closing o'er the fingers cold, on the lifeless pulseless
      breast,
The keen watching of His eyes, as He bends, as if
      addressed

To catch her first faint sigh !
Closer still, and yet more nigh
His face to hers.   So the mother o'er her sleeping child
Bends when the morning rays the eastern heavens gild.

My little one, mine own, awake !
Awake, my sweet one, for my sake !
As the babe wakes and laughs back into the mother's
face,
So wakes the fair dead maiden at that call of grace !

THE MAGI.

ISS the dimpled hands of the infant Christ,
        oh ye aged men !
    The first rippling smile of those baby
        lips is yours ; was it then
    For this ye came from far,
    Led by the prophetic star ?

O ye sages of the East ! wist ye that a little child,
The high gift of God could be ; discerned ye in that
        infant mild
    Our humanity's true king,
    Who the golden time should bring ?
Turning from the warrior king, with his pageantry of
        power,
To the virgin mother and the babe, in that quiet hour,

Saw ye not the uprising light
Of the day-spring infinite ?

Oh, the woes, the strife of earth, the voice of them
        that weep !
Hear ye not the bitter wailing voices from the deep ?
      Turn and look upon the child,—
      Look into those eyes so mild !

Oh, the shapings grand and dim, in the dreamy
        Eastern mind,
Of the great restoring one, this is He whom now ye find :
      Yea, behold a little child,
      Look into those eyes so mild !

JACOB'S DREAM.

 E slept, and over him the Syrian night
    Watched with her stars ; around, the
    mountains towered—
On stony pillow slept, far from the light
  Of the loved tent, spread where the trees embowered,
    Beside the smoothly-flowing streams
    Which glassed the morn and sunset beams !

Tier above tier the mighty hills uprose,
  Scaling the infinite skies—peak over peak,
Lifted aloft ; all solemn in repose,
  The lonely land : or ere the morning meek,
    Dropping cool dews advanced her way,
    To loose the massy gates of day !

The milky archway shot its lofty span
  Across the sapphire ; the great starry host
Clustered and burned on high—not pale and wan,
  As in our northern climes,—on heaven's high coast
    Fiery or golden, the great stars,
    Arcturus, Orion, Mars,
Shone glorious in the mazy train, and lit
  Th' illimitable vault.   On the stilled earth,
With her hushed creatures, a great awe did sit,
  Brooding as 'twere with covering wings : from forth
    That heart of silent mystery
    Issued no sound ; only a tree
Made o'er the sleeper's head a whisper low,
  With waving of its leaves.   Wearied he slept,
Forgetful of his toils and all the woe
  Which held his life in travail ; he had wept
    When from his father's house he turned,
    While still his rage within him burned
With smouldering fires half-quenched ; for he had bought
  The birthright, as he deemed, but might not take
The purchased prize, nor had he yet one thought
  How mean his craft, while still the wily snake

Of that great sin folded his heart,
With her foul coils o'er every part !

The glory of the heavenly doth arise
　Within the vision of the soul in dreams ;
Shadowed in likeness of the seen ; our eyes
　　But look on a thick veil, which hath no seams
　　　Nor any rent, but whole and one,
　　　Hangeth before the infinite sun !

We see the type ; but that which lies behind
　The type we faintly guess at.　There doth come,
Borne from afar, a whispering like the wind,
　　We hear, and name the spirit-voice ; the womb
　　　Of darkness darkly shuts us in,
　　　As creatures yet unborn, though thin

The fleshly covering which surrounds our being,
　And hides from us the spiritual.　We still
By sense discern the things above our seeing ;
　　Upward to God, and his ambrosial hill,
　　　We climb from the low sensual earth,
　　　As from dank mould the flower hath birth !

So in the mind of him that slept, the scene
 Of outer glory built itself anew
A spiritual grandeur; as upon a screen
 Reflected, the great heavenly splendours grew
  Within the mirror of that dream,
  Where mystic meanings thickly teem.

From the low earth, where lay the breathing things,
 Where the birds nestled, he beheld a glory,—
A ladder rising with great luminous rings,
 Piercing through the star-spaces white and hoary,—
  A starry ladder great and high,
  Reaching from earth unto the sky !

The lowest round bedded among the flowers,
 But the high topmost shaft hidden in God ;
And over it there fell the glory-showers
 Of angels : all along the golden road
  Passed to and fro the angelic throng,—
  The seraphs of the highest song !

And over it and up and down they passed
 Unceasing ; he beheld it with his eyes,
This dreamer of old time : along the vast
 Unbroken chain, immeasurable of size,

Ascending and descending moved,
God's chosen angels whom he loved!

He saw the astral radiance climb the skies,
   Stretching itself into the infinite,
As mountain peaks one after one arise,
   In a long chain of mounts,—in dazzling light,
      Went up the steps of those great stairs,
      Swept by the breath of heaven's own airs!

From the wet grasses where the young lambs lay
   Went up the glory, up to the high God.
Then saw he how that man might find a way,
   To the great heights by feet angelic trod,
      E'en to the heavenly throne above—
      A ladder knit with links of love!

How man might climb by steps of mountain-stairs
   Unto his Maker, and by starry rounds
Ascend; yea, from the lonely desert lairs
   Scale to the heavenly city's glorious bounds—
      The guarded and the sacred mount
      Whence blessings flow as from a fount!

THE BURIED TEMPLE.

N cavernous gloom,
Far under the earth,
A temple doth stand,
Duskily grand.
Perfect its pillars, and columns, and roof,
Exquisite, delicate traceries gleam on the walls,
Flowerets and fruitage woven in woof,
With the fan of the palm, and the fir trees' dark balls.

The pomegranates bloom
As when they had birth
In the carving's first glory,
In the dead cycles hoary.

Before the high altar the ancient priest waits ;
Dark raimented, mournful, and grand,
Keeping watch at the vast sculptured gates,
The old Hebrew prophets silently stand.

Never light of the sun,
Or the moon's pale beam,
Never throb of the star,
Trembling from far,
Doth shine on that temple so mighty and old.
In cavernous gloom of the deep hollow earth,
It uplifteth its great dome of gold,
There, where never a thing of beauty hath birth !

Not a motion or tone !
Like a weird dream,
The mute white priest,
The watchers at the east,
The prophets so stern with their grand stony gaze,
Immovable fixed ; changeless and still,
Huge shapes in that strange spectral haze,
They loom like the brow of a mist-circled hill !

In the times of the kings
Who made Israel to sin,
When the Gentile drew sword
In the land of the Lord,
When the fierce hosts rolled on like the billows that
    leap,
To slay and to spoil in the holy place,
The hard earth was cleft to its innermost deep,
And the temple sank, nor left a trace !.

Misty radiance rings
The dome—a thin
Pale belt of light—
Or else would night
Enshroud that mighty temple there.
The gates clang not, nor ever move,
Nor e'er is heard the voice of prayer,
Or music that the Hebrews love !

No breath, no sound
Of living thing :
Ghostly and dim
In the faint light's rim,

The temple of Solomon the wise !
Far down below the summer rills,
For ever hid from mortal eyes,
'Neath the foundations of the hills.

O'er the charmèd ground
No bird doth wing
Its flight, or ever
Its pinions quiver ;
No foot of man hath ever passed
The dim gigantic porch, or trod
The shadowy outer court, so vast,
Of that wondrous hidden house of God.

It standeth aye,
It hath no change ;
A mystery
No man may see.
So till the sublime word be given
To bid the buried grandeur rise ;
From the abyss it shall be riven
To tower in sunlight of the skies.

Glorious that day
Through earth's wide range,
From Afric's sands
To the cold northern lands.
The sea shall yield her precious things,
And give her jewels to bestrew the shores,
With low melodious murmurings
She shall pour forth her hidden stores.

On the great mount
Which God shall raise,
And with his hand
Make fair and grand—
With Carmel's grace, and Sinai's weird
Sublimity, with Lebanon's glory,
With cedars crowned—shall be upreared,
Grander than erst, that temple hoary !

Then the Talmudists count,
With its jewels ablaze,
Shall be brought forth,
Priceless in worth—

Q

The crown of the ancient Hebrew kings ;
And the Christ shall place it within the shrine :
There, 'neath the spread of the great seraph wings,
The circlet of David shall glitter and shine.

INDIA.

HE cry of babes and women—lo, we say,
Four millions hunger: can we part the lump
And take to heart each pining, wailing babe,
Each woman with wan lips, each gaunt worn man?
But God doth so, not we, for unto Him
Single the sparrow falls,
The half-fledged raven calls!

Sadder than all the battle-fields these deaths ;—
These women with dry breasts, dragged by the mouths
That fain would suck, are more to pain the heart
Than the fall'n warrior gashed with many wounds.
And shall we let them die, we who are set
The foremost of the earth
To lead Christ's kingdom forth?

The iron wheels of nature roll and grind
Her faultful peoples ; say they have not learned
Aright her laws, for she hath warned and bid
Them take the larger foresight to provide
Against the evil, but they lived, as lives

      The insect in the bower,
      Fluttering its little hour

We too are shallow : we have heaped all filth,
All scum within our midst, till the keen sword
Smote for our sin, and with rash hand have let
Our human jewels in our gutters drop,
Our unowned children sink in hells of slush.

      The curse of broken law
      Is ours—stand we in awe !

Oh people ! mighty in the days of old,
Whose sages in the dim gray dawn of time
Fronted with lifted brows the uprising sun,
Ye were a glory in the ancient earth,
And from your lofty natures did evolve

      A creed sublime and grand
      When barbarous was our land.

Yet to be great hereafter, when we wed,
In golden marriage with your antique race,
The vigour of our new, our western strength,
With all that dreamy sweetness which is soul
Of eastern life ; no longer twain that day,
　　　But one, by the great hand
　　　Of God conjoined, we stand !

Then shall the kingdom of the future rise,
Like the fine vision of the heavenly mount
Within the prophet's mind—the city of God,
Wherein no evil thing shall come, from whence
Through open gates pour forth the glorious hosts,
　　　From the great throne, God's river,
　　　For. ever and for ever !

August, 1877.

THE ADVENT.

OD'S greatest, oh Thou little child !
    Man's least,—laid with the beasts in stall.
In the high round of heaven the battalions
        bright
    Sang Thee, earth's new-born King !

The shepherds watching o'er their flocks
    Saw rising on the dark the sheen
Of Seraph wings, and heard that mighty song
    As torrent waters rolled !

Heard they through the great host the song
    Roll on, as trumpet-echoes blown
From cliff to cliff in the deep hollowed heart
    Of mountains in a ring !

Kiss ye the azure-tinted lids
Of the meek babe, rocked to its sleep
Upon the virgin breast ; ye shepherds, bend
And worship the young child !

And now we listen, but, alas !
We hear no waft of angel-song,
But shouts of them that strive, the dying groans,
The fallen war-steeds' cries.

The sullen cannon's deadly roar,
And the red leap of angry flame,
The mangled bodies, and the smoking towns,
These are the things that be.

And from across the Eastern seas
The voice of weeping for the dead,
The Indian Rachel mourning for her sons :
Oh Thou great God, how long !

And yet each day is born anew,
In meekness and in lowliness,
The Christ of God into our world, in shapes
Diverse and multiform.

In deeds of love, of purity,
    In all self sacrifice, in all
Great striving after truth, in him who toils,
        Or him who quietly thinks.

In him who does a servant's work,
    In him who lifts the statesman's voice,
In those who meekly suffer, without word
        To speak their suffering.

God's mystery of power is shut
    Into low forms, or such we deem
Low forms, yet ever to His clearer eyes
        The inner glory shines.

And some there be that hear e'en now
    The song of the Great Seraphin
Floating adown the silences of night,—
        This night of our earth's woe!

Peal out, and louder, heavenly song,
    Burst on our ears this Christmas morn,
On God's high hills ye sing, oh Seraphin!
        The Christ new born to men.

Christmas, 1877.

THE NEST.

 FOUND a lark's nest yesterday,
    I found it in the grass, on the low ground,
        But in the sapphire heights above
The spirit bird, the lark, did make a sound

    Of music, raining down a flood
Of song. On the low ground it had its nest ;
        But in the heart of highest heaven
It poured full tide of glorious song : the rest

    So lowly, but the song so high.
Oh bird, oh voice, oh living melody !
        Is it because you build so low
You soar so high ? Is thy great ecstacy

Fed from the low earth-source? and hath
The dim sweet mystery of folded life
   In yon small nest filled all thine heart,
Until it overbrims in song so rife

   Of joy, so jubilant, so wild?
I know not ; it may be all joy, all love,
   Have lowly source : that earthly love
Feeds that which is divine.   To heights above

   All measure love and joy ascend,
Which yet have fountain in most lowly place :
   No poet song but hath its spring
In simplest thing ; the sweet home-life doth trace

   Outward its deep divinity
In patriot and sage ; no love of child
   But hath its growth toward largest love
Of man.   All loves, all feelings soft and mild,

   Do cluster like the sweet rose-leaves
Round the red core, about one central love ;
   So mounts the soul on lark-like wings,
So sings, like thee, oh bird ! in heaven above.

MAY.

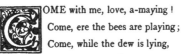 OME with me, love, a-maying !
 Come, ere the bees are playing;
 Come, while the dew is lying,
And cloud with cloud is vying,
  And lightly floating by,
  In the soft morning sky.
  Come to the flowery mead,
  Where the sweet pleasures lead
The airy dance and mirthful song,
For ever fair and ever young;
   Come, love, with me !

Sit with me, love, a-maying,
'Neath the white branches swaying,

Where the young violet, dying,
Sends out her soul in sighing,
 And breathes of nought but love,
 To the rapt breeze above.
 Here, on a flowery bed,
 Mine heart to thine I'd wed,
And all the sweetness of the May
Pour out in many a tender lay,
 My love, to thee !

THE MOTHER'S PRAYER.

SHE moved from the ranks of the shining
   ones,
  That mother saintly and white,
She stood at the feet of the Lord of life,
 She stood in the angels' sight,
And unto the heavenly King she said :
 " Oh Father, that lovest all,
I hear the cry of my child in the earth—
 I hear my little one call !
The little one weepeth sore," she said ; -
 " He was my joy ; my breast
Did give him suck, my voice at night
 Did lull him into rest ;

But now no hands do fondle him,
   My babe, my tender one !
No eyes do kindle his to smiles,
   My lambkin weak and lone !
Let me go to tend mine hapless babe,
   Till the days when he shall stand
A man 'mong men, noble and strong—
   Let me to yon dim land,
For this return, Father of all ! "
   So prayed ; and the angel bands
Made pause of song to hear what the Lord
   Should speak, then laid He His hands
On her saintly head, and said : " Not so ;
   My daughter abide thou still,
In the realms of light, 'mong my holy ones,
   Tarry thou here secure from ill."
" The little one needeth me," she said ;
   " Let me go to tend my child,
For I know that he must suffer woe,
   In life so rough and wild.
The young child weepeth sore," she said ;
   " Let me shield my tender one

From the storm and blast of the bitter earth,

    Till the days of trial be done."

Then the Lord made answer unto her :

    " Oh woman, not so ! behold,

I work my ends through ill to good ;

    Through the damp and heavy mould,

The shafted leaves do push to life,

    From the seed which dies below,

The spiritual flower doth rise and grow,

    With sun-dyed hues aglow !

And through the shapings manifold

    Of suffering and pain,

The human growth attains its end ;

    Nothing is void, nor vain,

For evil doth work the work of good."

REST.

HE Christ was sleeping.
    On His great amplitude of brow was peace,
        And smiles upleaping
On the calm lips.   Hath He awhile found ease,

       The Man of Sorrows?
Hath His great heart fore-gone its bitter toil,
       And bliss, which borrows
All heaven, in dreams, come to Him without soil?

       The waves up-heaving
Break not His rest; the tempest ploughs the deep,
       The wild winds cleaving
Wildly their way over the waters' sweep,

But He is resting,—
The Man who wept, who suffered, toiled, and loved ;
He, who, divesting
Himself of glory, among men still moved,

Their changeless lover,
Working to ends of changeless love, now rests.
The storm sweeps over
The vexed and harried deep ; their white foam crests

The waves are rearing.
Around the sleeping Christ amazed they stand ;
Such terrors wearing,
The scene appals their hearts.   Why doth His hand

Lie thus all nerveless ?
The hand which grasped the seed-germs of the world,
Which guided, swerveless,
The great life-forces, when all forms unfurled

To life and beauty.
Peace, ye, and wake Him not.   O slow of heart!

R

        The higher duty
Is faith in that ineffable calm.   Your part,

        O unbelieving !
Is meek reposing in the unbounded love,
        From it receiving
Peace in the paths where storm and tempest move.

HE GIVETH HIS BELOVED SLEEP.

HE sleeps ; we would not wake her—no !
God hushed her to her rest, with low
Whisperings of love. Oh, sleep, not

death—
Call it not death !—sweet sleep, life's wreath,
  And crown of balmiest blessing !

For whom the Highest loveth best,
He earliest gathers to His breast.
Like shadowing of an angel's wing,
Soft as the shade, when the young Spring,
  With sweet flowers the earth dressing,

Brings over it an April cloud,
Fell that soft balm of rest.   The loud

And turbulent life doth vex our souls :
The mad world's crashing thunder-rolls
    Of battle ; the wild sad moaning

Of an ever-heaving sea of doubt,
Which swathes our isle of life about :
For alway in the mist we stand,
And see not clear His face and hand,
    Who loveth us, still groaning

"He hath forsaken," though He love,
E'en as a mother loves.   Sweet dove,
Thou hast found rest within His breast !
Into the calm art passed, and bless'd
    With Christ's own face uplifted,

Rejoicest evermore.   Oh flower !
Oh lily of our hearts, thine hour
Was come ! He saw thy bloom, and took
Thee for His lily.   Now we look
    On thy bare place.   But shifted

Art thou, sweet flower, from earth to heaven ;
For unto thee such grace is given,
To live, dear one, within His sight,
To grow in beauty stainless white,
　　Breathing for Him thy sweetness.

Yea, we shall miss thee much ; our tears
Must flow ; and through the long slow years
Our grief must live, so dear wast thou :
Yet the great peace upon thy brow,
　　And thy young soul's full meetness

For Christ and heaven, forbid our grief,
Else wild ; and but a moment brief,
And the thin veil of this our life
Shall part, and we beyond the strife,
　　The turmoil and the weeping

Shall pass, and find thee yet again
Our own ; and all the bitter pain
Pass into joy.   Meanwhile, rest thou
Beneath the shadowing of God's brow,
　　Safe in His holy keeping !

NOTES.

BALDER.

Page 183, lines 1, 2.

"Yet shall he come again and build his throne
In Asgard, when the days are ripe," etc.

HE story of Balder the Beautiful is well known. The goddess Frigga being apprehensive for the fate of her son, took an oath of everything in creation not to do him harm, the mistletoe alone excepted, possibly on account of its insignificance. Loki, the evil one, the contriver of mischief against the gods, having discovered this, causes a shaft made of the mistletoe to be aimed at Balder by one of his companions. The missile effects his death, and as he dies ingloriously, he falls under the dominion of Hela, the goddess of the dead. The mission of Hermode, who is despatched to effect his release, proving a failure through a certain old woman in a cave (who is supposed to be Loki in disguise) refusing to afford the tribute of tears which every other creature gives, he remains under the power of the pale goddess of the shades until the end of time, when it is predicted he will return from the dismal halls of Hela and resume his former glory, restoring the earth, which has been desolated, and establishing universal peace and happiness.

Balder resembles in some respects Apollo, the sun-god of the Greeks, and in others may be compared to Sosiosh, the redeemer, of the Persian system. He is the god of eloquence, of music, and of poetry, so fair and beautiful in person that rays of light issue from his forehead, adorning it with a crown of sun-rays. Like the Greek Apollo he endures a long exile from the abodes of the gods.

The myth is one of the finest of the many really fine things of the Northern mythology. In its primary significance it is like most of the myths of the old religions, a shadow from the outward and external on the mind of men. The restoration of the god from the doleful shades of Hela is the emergence of the sun in its morning glory from the gloom of night, or the return of spring to the earth after the rigours of winter; and this, grand in its conception as it would appear to the people of the cold Northern clime, has, beyond this, a certain deeper and more spiritual meaning : it speaks of a hope of immortality, of a life utterly imperishable and divine, which must loose the bands of death because it is not possible it should be holden of them.

There is nothing finer in its way than the story of Balder in the whole range of Persian, Hindostanic, or Hellenic myths.

THE BURIED TEMPLE.

Page 209, lines 1—3.

" In cavernous gloom,
Far under the earth,
A temple doth stand."

There is a tradition in the Talmud that the Temple of
Solomon is still existent, concealed in the depths of the
earth ; and that when the nation of Israel shall be again
restored to their own land, it will re-appear as perfect as
when first erected on Mount Zion.

At the taking of Jerusalem by Sennacherib, the Rabbis
believe the Temple, by the Ministry of Angels, was pre-
served from destruction by being hidden beneath the
earth, where it still remains.

7 2

Lightning Source UK Ltd.
Milton Keynes UK
UKOW05f1403060217

293731UK00001B/77/P